SEAFARERES IN TROUBLED WATERS

SEAFARERS IN TROUBLED WATERS

*Establishing a paradigm shift conducive
to improved mental health on board*

FENNA KLEBERT

Bibliografische Information der Deutschen Nationalbibliothek:
Die Deutsche Nationalbibliothek verzeichnet diese Publikation
in der Deutschen Nationalbibliografie; detaillierte bibliografische Daten sind im Internet über dnb.dnb.de abrufbar.

Herstellung und Verlag: BoD – Books on Demand, Norderstedt

ISBN: 978-3-7568-3675-8

PREFACE   7

MAYDAY MAYDAY, CAN YOU HEAR US?   9

State of Research   11

Stakeholder   12

Organisation on Board   15

SITUATION ON BOARD   17

Mental Health   18

Healthcare on Board   20

Factor Loneliness   22

Factors Leadership and Group   24

Interim Conclusion: The Human Factor   26

BUSINESS MANAGEMENT APPROACHES   28

Diversity Management   29

Team   31

Leadership Approaches   36
   Transformational Leadership   37
   Shared Leadership and Hierarchy   41
   Feel Good Management   46

RECOMMENDATIONS FOR HR MANAGEMENT   48

Onboarding   49

Staff Appraisal   52
    Introductory and Final Discussion   53
    Appraisal Interview   55

WHO WILL ANSWER THE CALL?   59

PREFACE

The present work is late in every respect. And yet it is as topical as ever. Inspired by the author's personal experience in active seafaring, the next pages should inspire and empower many people.

All people who participate in global world trade as soon as they enter a supermarket or an electronics store, yet know little of the most important transportation system that keeps everything moving, maritime shipping.

All personnel managers, whether in maritime crewing or in other industries which demand more from employees than what the already overstrained working environment requires. Sometimes it is the smaller things that can change an entire organisation for the better (or for the worse).

All decision-makers ashore in the maritime industry who manage the fate of the shipping companies and thus the ships which sail the seas, thereby indirectly and directly determining the lives of the people on board every single day.

And not to forget, the most important group of stakeholders, all seafarers who are confronted with physical and technical challenges day after day. Who deal with their challenges in a highly professional manner. May this book give them the inspiration to understand their environment as a social challenge and to treat it accordingly.

This book can only be the beginning of something. It does not offer a complete solution, nor can it reform the entire human resources policy of the maritime industry. It is a discursive contribution to a change of mindset that is very slowly taking hold of this industry and putting people at the center; initially from a technical perspective, to be sure, but increasingly from a social one as well. From this point, we must continue to think, act, revise and improve. This applies to science as well as to practice.

I would therefore like to thank all the people who accompanied me especially in the early years of my professional career and who (for better or worse) have had a lasting impact on my understanding of teamwork, leadership, and togetherness. May the central idea of human-centered, dignified shipping inspire your growth.

Without a doubt, professions in the maritime industry are among the most exciting you can imagine. A real paradigm shift could convince more people of this.

Mayday Mayday, can you hear us?

"SOS on Christmas Eve" was the headline of the German news magazine SPIEGEL ONLINE on Christmas Eve 2020, recalling the hundreds of thousands of seafarers who were cut off from their homes in the wake of the global Covid-19 pandemic. A much overdue article, in which the author Stefan Kruecken himself states that the majority of goods are transported by sea freight, but that awareness of the working conditions on board merchant ships among consumers is close to zero.[2] However, the author disregards two points. Firstly, seafarers in what is known as "christliche Seefahrt" (English: Christian Seafaring) in German speaking countries, is by no means exclusively affiliated with the churches, so that Christmas stands out as a special event in the year for all of them. And secondly, even more seriously, the events at the end of 2020 reveal a system in which there is little space and hardly any resonance for the people at sea - 365 days a year.

Global maritime shipping is an incomparable industry. Although some of the many maritime stakeholders will be identified in the course of this work, the focus will be on the entity *ship* as the smallest possible organisational unit. The crew within their living and working environment represents the most elementary part of maritime shipping, as it is the key factor in the successful functioning of the ship as an entity and therefore the industry as a whole: "[...] a ship is a complex human-machine system, an interwoven set of sociotechnical systems, and human interaction is a crucial factor for the safe and efficient operation of the ship."[3] A complex, interlocking system that is susceptible to failure precisely because of the indispensable human factor - human error is identified as the cause of a large proportion of all more or less serious shipping accidents. In addition, the maritime shipping industry has a higher mortality rate than comparative groups due to accidents, illnesses and suicides, as this publication will show.[4] From a business perspective, the consequences are not only loss of material or disruptions to the voyage. With every extraordinary loss of staff, know-how is lost and at least costs are incurred through return transport and the replacement of the workforce at short notice. It therefore seems advisable to focus more consistently on the individual physical and psychological needs of the members of the ship's crew in order to create respectful conditions for them.

The following pages will therefore begin with a scientific classification and a systematic and problem-oriented presentation of the situation on board. The aim of this is to establish the human being as the subject of the following considerations. In the second part, organisational approaches will be used; both diversity management and leadership concepts will be taken into account in order to approach job satisfaction as an objective of personnel policy-making decisions. This is followed by the concretisation in the form of two design recommendations that could significantly shape cooperation on board. Finally, this transfer to the maritime world of work should encourage the industry to rethink outdated structures and labour policy measures that have only managed to persist in maritime shipping.

State of Research

At the beginning of the research, it became clear that the academic disciplines primarily concerned in the German-speaking world (namely nautical science and shipping management) have surprisingly little research interest in the problematic management of human labour on board. The book "Suizid und Männlichkeit. Selbsttötungen von Männern auf See, in der Wehrmacht und im zivilen Bereich, 1893- ca. 1986" about suicide aboard by the humanities scholar Nicole Schweig will not have much influence on the content, but it is a good example of how this obviously explosive topic is mostly tackled by authors from outside the original maritime sciences. Therefore, publications from various disciplines form the basis, whereby the particularly promising works mostly come from anglophone academia. Last but not least, the sources are confirmed or supplemented in some places by personal experiences that both the author of this book herself, as a former ship mechanic at sea, and members of the profession on board merchant ships interviewed by her were able to gather.

A number of studies will also be noted as a much-appreciated basis for all further strands of thought. Two of these have been commissioned by the International Transport Workers' Federation (ITF, based in London): The 2016 report on seafarers' mental health[5] was followed in 2019 by a comprehensive study[6] by US medical experts Rafael Lefkowitz and Martin Slade. The book edited by psychologist Malcolm MacLachlan, which also involved some captains,[7] will also provide insights and perspectives on mental health care on board. In addition, it is important to refer to the publication "Human Factors in the Maritime Domain" by the Australian Michelle R. Grech et al. which, although more than fifteen years old, refers very precisely and critically to the way cost-fixated shipping deals with its employees.[8] More recently, Jürgen Neff (ed.) deals with the human (safety) factor in maritime shipping.[9] This book will also find its way into the present work, with some exceptions, as it relates exclusively to the crew of bridges.

In addition to the "human factor", the topic of "decent work" is also introduced. In this context, the contribution by the economist Heide Gerstenberger in the anthology by Guido Becke et al.[10] "The Wiley Blackwell Handbook of the Psychology of Team Working and Collaborative Processes" by Eduardo Salas et al. also contains a promising contribution on group performance in extreme situations, which can be transferred well to the ship situation.[11] A multi-faceted approach to the "International Dimensions of Organisational Behaviour" is provided in the book by the US economist Nancy J. Adler.[12]

The onboarding process, which is presented as one of the proposals for action at the end of the book, is a young and therefore not yet widely discussed approach. It is for this reason that the author relies mainly on the publications of economist Doris Brenner[13] on the one hand and the economists around Klaus Moser[14] on the other. The various manifestations of employee interviews are introduced with the help of the business economists around Wolfgang Mentzel[15] and the economic and organisational psychologist Oswald Neuberger.

Stakeholder

As already indicated at the beginning, the maritime business operates as an extremely complex and global system in which the seafarers themselves are only granted a rather passive role. Contacting individual stakeholders proved to be difficult not only in the course of this study, but also for other researchers; other studies also complain that the willingness of shipping companies or insurers to provide data was limited.[16] However, in order to provide as detailed a picture as possible of the environment in which the ship moves as an organisational unit, some of the maritime industry's interest groups will be presented.

First and foremost are the **seafarers**. Worldwide, around 1.6 million men and women work on seagoing vessels (as of 2017);[17] on German merchant ships with a total of around 8200 employees, just over 500 are female and mainly work in the service sector.[18] This is by no means a homogeneous group, neither in its entirety nor in the ship as a place to live and work. As Annika Schellbach also suggests,[19] crews must be regarded as a highly diversified group, especially in terms of age structure, religious and cultural identity and (despite a low proportion of women) gender and sexual orientation. Transport language on board is mostly English, which can be a barrier to the health care discussed below. In addition, very different employment conditions and changing workplaces (classic regular occupations are a rare phenomenon, at least in global merchant shipping) make networking or even the establishment of workers' representations difficult.

This in turn affects the work of the **trade unions**. In Germany, the trade union *ver.di* represents the interests of German employees in the maritime and port industries. However, the mandate is not a particularly large one, given a traditionally rather sceptical attitude of German seafarers towards trade unions; only a few shipping companies have a trade union friendly climate, mostly in ferry companies. This is why the focus will be on the internationally active (not only, but also) seafarers' union ITF, which has commissioned the above-mentioned comprehensive studies. It has also been at the forefront of the fight against the archaic working conditions in the maritime shipping industry, especially since the start of the pandemic in 2020. ITF is also represented as an NGO in the International Maritime Organization (IMO), a specialised agency within the UN, where it primarily campaigns for safety and labour rights issues.[20]

Unfortunately, more often than not, the **shipping companies**, as well as – partly in-house – **crewing agencies** (which provide and place seafaring personnel worldwide), act as a contrary force in relation to a positive work environment on board. By outsourcing crew acquisition and management as well as deployment planning to these crewing agencies, the link between the maritime personnel and the shipping companies they ultimately work for is missing. Classical shipping companies, as Gerstenberger points out, no longer exist, as ownership and operation of a ship is now often the responsibility of different companies. Rather, cost-fixed chartering is the main factor determining the day-to-day business and the company's policies, so that, for example, possible safety concerns on board are relegated to the background when decisions are made about the itinerary.[21] Germany continues to see itself as a "Schifffahrtsstandort" (a term used to emphasise a strong heritage of maritime expertise and tradition, coupled with know-how and the famed German quality of engineering) and makes this clear, among other things, through a foundation of the same name.[22] In fact, even after the devastating financial crisis of 2008, there are still over 300 shipping companies as represented by the German Shipowners' Association *Verband Deutscher Reeder* (VDR). However, this belies the fact that only about 43% of the ships reported are sailing under the European flag.[23] Moreover, it is not possible to draw any conclusions from this as to what the labour and living conditions on board are like. For example, the majority of flag states allow seafarers to be employed at the local wage rate. This means that even a European ship does not guarantee payment to non-European seafarers at European rates; rather, the wage level in the seafarers' countries of origin is the basis. The control of all regulations is the responsibility of the **classification societies** and **flag state** on the one hand, and **authorities** such as the port states on the other. In 2019, port state inspections revealed more than 3200 deficiencies in working and living conditions in the 27 states subject to the Paris Memorandum of Understanding alone.[24] However, the close economic network of these stakeholders with the shipping companies themselves suggests that critical situations on board are not always assessed objectively. Both the classification societies (quasi the Technical Inspection Association TÜV for seagoing vessels) and the flag states compete for the shipping companies' orders and are paid for their services.

From a financial point of view in particular, the **maritime insurers** appear as further protagonists who organise themselves in P&I clubs. The scope of this book does not allow for a deeper look into the details of the contractual modalities; moreover, the insurance agencies surveyed did not provide any information on how the costs of lost time injury could be quantified. Nevertheless, it can be concluded that there is an increased interest in a humane working environment. Helen Sampson and Neil Ellis, in their survey of employers and insurance companies, found that the latter were more aware of the mental strain on seafarers than shipowners, even though they did not pursue any concrete courses of action.[25]

Up to this point, it can be said that global merchant shipping has many internationally active protagonists. All of them have an impact on the crews with their different requirements and thus influence the actions of those responsible and consequently the well-being of the seafarers.

Organisation on Board

In 2020, the global merchant fleet consisted of over 55,000 ships, with general and bulk carriers leading the statistics by ship type in terms of numbers and deadweight tonnage.[26] For this reason, too, the crew of a bulk carrier will be used as an example for further considerations.

The IMO's "Principles of Minimum Safe Manning" were adopted in 2011 and provide for ship-dependent manning numbers and structures. The respective flag state in turn determines, on the basis of the IMO regulation, which minimum manning must be covered by rank when setting sail. Depending on the interpretation, two or three working areas can be identified on board a cargo ship: While the technical *engine department* is usually perceived as a single unit, the *bridge department* could be regarded as independent of the *deck department*, with the employees on deck often receiving their tasks from the bridge team.

Thus, the nautical, i.e., bridge crew of the exemplary ship could consist of a master and two watch officers (chief mate and second mate) manning the bridge at sea in a 24-hour watch system. Similarly, one ship engineer (Chief Engineer) is responsible for the technical aspects (beyond the engine room) of mechanical and electrical matters throughout the vessel. This is supported by an additional engineer (2nd Engineer) as well as a motor woman. Engine rooms of smaller ships do not have to be manned around the clock, nor can this be guaranteed in view of the crew size, so that alarm systems are installed on the cabin of the technical staff. Formally, the deck crew is headed by a boatswain, but often this position is now held by a sailor without the expectation of a corresponding salary. The bosun is usually given duties by the Chief Mate and delegates these to two deckhands (Able-bodied Seaman (A.B.) and Ordinary Seaman (O.S.)). A cook is supposed to take care of the physical well-being. On smaller units, this person is often also assigned on deck.

More or less friendly rivalries can be observed on many ships, especially between the engine team and the bridge team, which sometimes, however, lead to open conflicts.[27] The final decision making power, with the associated legal consequences and binding force, lies with the captain. In reality, however, at least two positions of personnel responsibility can be identified, as both the chief engineer and the first officer order activities and control their fulfilment. For this reason, leadership responsibility and personnel care cannot be considered the sole monopoly of the captain. They also act as an interface with other stakeholders, first and foremost the shipping company itself and the authorities at the ports of call and must therefore implement their decisions and be accountable to the crew. Here too, as the following work will show, communication cannot be a one-way street. The holistic view of the microcosm of the ship therefore does not allow for a one-sided perception of a centralised leadership figure.

Situation on Board

For every seafarer, the ship is both a workplace and a temporary home. While there is currently much discussion about the blurring of boundaries through home offices in times of pandemics, a separation on board, between the two, seems spatially and mentally unrealisable. In view of months of on-board operations, the results of the study by Sampson and Ellis seem all the more alarming: "Although many seafarers seem to cope surprisingly well with challenging psycho-social issues on board (indicating remarkable levels of resilience in the face of assault and bullying, for example) they are significantly more likely to feel happy at home than at sea."[28] Now, "being happy" is not synonymous with mental health. Nevertheless, this finding is worrying, especially in view of the considerable imbalance between deployment and leave, particularly among non-European seafarers. For example, Filipino employees often come on board for nine months or more, only to return to their families unpaid for a few weeks. Different conditions are known to apply to German seafarers. On ships under the German flag or in particularly lucrative sectors such as the offshore segment 1:1 contracts are possible, according to which, for example, two weeks of work are followed by the same amount of leave. In contrast ratios of 2:1 or even 3:1 between deployment and leave time have become established in the global cargo shipping industry.

Based on a number of scientific studies, this chapter will focus on the mental health of seafarers as a cause of absenteeism, although physical influences will by no means be completely ignored. From this, individual factors will be extracted that also have an impact on the image of people in the maritime industry and have a lasting influence on the environment.

Mental Health

Mental health is a taboo subject aboard - even more so than in civil society in general. The reasons for this are manifold but can certainly also be attributed to an outdated understanding of masculinity in the predominantly masculine environment. The psychologist MacLachlan identifies five "challenges and opportunities for maritime psychology", i.e., sticking points that, in his view, should be given special consideration.[29] The two challenges of *ship evacuation* (especially on passenger ships) and *piracy*[30] are always present subliminally, but should be neglected because they are not organisational in origin. MacLachlan, however, also cites "organisational culture" and studies that plead for a particular kind of togetherness on board that not only takes diversity into account but also makes use of it to create value.[31] This book will also pursue this approach below. First, however, the two defining points according to MacLachlan, "Psychological Capital" and "Global Health at Work", will be examined in more detail. The "PsyCap" (according to Luthans et al.) should be established alongside the social and financial value of work, as it also (in the best case) contributes positively to productivity. To achieve this, a safer working climate must be created.[32] In addition, the congruence of life and work makes it indispensable to consider health and health care comprehensively and to include non-communicable diseases.[33] According to the author, it is not only language barriers that make it difficult to detect mental illnesses and crises, but also the reluctance to open up to superiors or colleagues. There is an urgent need for action in the maritime sector.

Lefkowitz and Slade also show that seafarers (especially on container ships) are more affected by depression than other occupational groups.[34] 20% of the respondents in the study stated that they had suicidal thoughts with varying frequency.[35] At the same time, 35% of depressed seafarers would not ask anyone for help and a vanishingly small minority would seek professional help. Only the destigmatisation of mental illnesses could lead to an open culture of conversation on board and thus counteract the risk of suicide, according to the medical experts.[36]

Like MacLachlan, the medical doctor Marcus Oldenburg and the psychologist Hans-Joachim Jensen point to a variety of circumstances that affect maritime personnel and, according to their findings, lead to "psychosocial stress".[37] They name eight factors that need to be taken into account:[38]

- The watch system, which does not coincide with the natural day-night rhythm.
- Exhaustion, which is favoured by sometimes short and labour-intensive port lay times and is also reflected in the accident statistics.
- The separation from family and social environment ashore, which leads to a one-sided social role on board and a feeling of non-participation in life on land.
- The physical influences such as "temperature, humidity, noise levels and vibration", which always and particularly in bad weather have an effect on the body.
- The high risk of coming to harm at work or at heavy sea.
- The increased work demands at all ranks, which are mainly due to time pressure.
- The extreme crisis situations that seafarers always face, e.g., with the potential ship total loss or the threat of piracy.
- The international composition of the crews, which makes communication difficult, contributes to further conflicts and to the feeling of isolation.

In addition, the use of an ever-increasing number of monitoring systems for the purpose of boosting efficiency is becoming the norm, making permanent remote monitoring of all technical components of a ship possible. It can be assumed that this will put additional pressure on the sailing personnel, as constant feedback from the shore creates an ongoing justification situation.

In this environment, not only largely undetected mental illnesses thrive. In order to counteract the abuse of intoxicants on board, some employers have adopted a zero-alcohol policy, with the result that the social component of communal celebrations[39] is increasingly disappearing. Whether the motives of the firms are exclusively aimed at the health of the seafarers cannot be determined at this point. It is indisputable that alcohol continues to be a dominant issue on board and a cause of accidents.[40] At the same time, the misuse of narcotics is also an outlet and thus a sign of personal overload and a lack of levelling alternatives.

Healthcare on Board

Merchant ships are equipped with a small infirmary and an onboard pharmacy, the stock of which exceeds international standards, depending on the flag state. A watch officer is responsible for the inventory and dispensing of less potent medicines, but also for the treatment of minor injuries or illnesses, depending on the safe manning. The strong opioids carried on board, on the other hand, are kept under lock and key by the captain in case of emergency. If necessary, the navigators are supported by medical handbooks and radio medical advisory services.

In any case, it is questionable to what extent the superficial basic medical training of the bridge team in the course of nautical studies is sufficient to provide well-founded emergency and health care on board. Firstly, the quality is strongly dependent on the individual motivation of the officer. Secondly, a look at the module handbooks of the four nautical colleges in Germany makes it clear that health care is often thought of only somatically and dealt with in only one module. The university curriculum also includes a hospital internship lasting a few weeks. Every five years, German navigators are required to renew their medical knowledge in a course.

A medical emergency is therefore one of the worst-case scenarios on board a merchant ship on a global voyage. This applies even more to mental crises and illnesses. This is why the ITF study of 2016 also suggests adding the module "mental health" to medical training, since the "extension of this model to the area of mental health has been proven to not only increase mental health literacy among participants but also to change beliefs about treatment, decrease social distancing and stigma about people with mental disorders, and increase the amount of help provided to others."[41] So far, there is a lack of sound knowledge about the identification and treatment of mental illnesses as well as an atmosphere in which personal weaknesses can be openly admitted. Furthermore, it cannot be assumed that there is a relationship of trust between doctors and patients, as is customary in other branches ashore. There is a considerable inconsistency here due to the employee-provider relationship, which makes open communication almost impossible.

Up to this point, various challenges that affect the crew of a ship could be compiled. It would go beyond the scope of this book to take all of them equally into account. The goal of making concrete measures for establishing social competence on board theoretically usable therefore requires a focussed approach. In the further course, the social isolation of the individual and the importance of leadership within the ship community will be problematised. This will provide a basis for selected business management points of reference from human resources and diversity management.

Factor Loneliness

Loneliness is a consequence of social isolation, which the ITF study of 2016 also problematises: "Social isolation arises from actual or perceived separation from others with whom open and supportive communication can take place. Social isolation is most likely to occur in settings where people are deprived of satisfying social contact."[42] Unsatisfactory or missing social exchange leads to anger, frustration, and sadness, among others. According to this, "rapid technological advancement, increased automation, reduced manning levels, ever more diverse crews, limited shore leave, faster turnaround times, and a naturally hierarchical command structure" act as a kind of accelerant for such critical conditions on board of seagoing vessels.[43]

Time and again, studies such as this one conclude that the effects of changed staffing policies (reduced and more diverse crews) are to be measured at different levels. The reduced workforce on board inevitably affects weekly working hours, but also the strained supervisor-employee relationship and social life. A constructive discussion needs to be initiated in the maritime business community in which the pressure of the cost factor labour - so far too little questioned - is yielded to. However, this book aims to elicit concrete recommendations for onboard life, so that such debates can only remain a side note.

It is alarming how isolation affects the mental health of seafarers. This is also the conclusion of the Chinese study by Quili Hui, where it is imperative to counteract loneliness. According to this study, team sports and sporting activities in general are an effective means of promoting togetherness.[44] This view is shared by Sampson and Ellis, who call on shipping companies to offer a "varied menu of interactive recreational activities."[45]

In addition to the changed crew structure, the dynamics of global maritime trade also have an indirect effect on the psyche of the sailing personnel. Oldenburg and Jensen published another study in 2019 entitled "Maritime welfare facilities - Utilization and relevance for the compensation of shipboard stress".[46] Qualitative research was conducted on the compensatory significance of shore leave and its risk due to the work rhythm in the feeder transport sector, i.e., on small ships that call at many ports at very short intervals. The work load, poor access to local facilities (seafarers' missions, localities, shopping facilities) and limited information channels would make regular visits ashore difficult.[47] The two researchers conclude that "maritime welfare facilities constitute an important refuge for seafarers beyond their ships to recover from demanding work and to 'recharge their batteries'."[48] In this study, too, breaking out of the one-sided social role constituted by the ship is significant for the seafarers,[49] for whom going ashore also provides the opportunity to make contact with their families, for example in internet cafés. Maintaining social land contacts thus remains one of the greatest challenges, so that Sampson and Ellis, for example, clearly plead for free and unrestricted access to the internet.[50] Up to now, many shipping corporations have shied away from the cost of satellite-based options. Lefkowitz and Slade even find a direct connection between digital infrastructure and physical illness: "While frequency of internet and email access was not associated with statistically significant differences in the depression or anxiety distribution, more frequent email and internet was associated with decreased likelihood of suicidal ideation".[51]

However, the proposed measures cannot hide the fact that the crew encompasses the primary social environment during an onboard assignment. It has already been pointed out several times that the overlap between the living space and the working world is considerable. Psychologist Claudia Vaupel therefore clearly points out the very limited privacy on board.[52] Opportunities for retreat are limited (even temporarily) and, as mentioned, offer little compensation and often only more loneliness. Radio and television, but also inexpensive and constantly available opportunities to make phone calls are not offered in most cases. It is therefore all the more important to reform social life on board and to respond more sensitively than before to individual needs. To this end, the traditional hierarchical structuring must also be taken into account, which often enough stands in the way of informal togetherness.

Factors Leadership and Group

On board ships, without known exception, a hierarchical system is maintained. The ranks described at the beginning are therefore not only an expression of qualification and a job description, but also refer to the respective person's place in the social structure. Often, in addressing people, the name disappears behind the rank designation, this determines in which mess hall (canteen) the person may eat and on which deck as well as how comfortably they are placed. Rank also influences social interaction through a distinctive structure of those authorised to issue instructions and those receiving instructions. In such an environment, personal relationships develop only sparsely and mostly only between persons of one language area.

It can be said that an often-authoritarian style of leadership on board has a severe impact on everyone's life and work. This does not only affect people in the lower ranks. In the survey by Bjorn Mast,[53] 13% of the officers interviewed cited pressure as a trigger for negative feelings, as well as a lack of teamwork (11%), poor relationships with others (8%) and loneliness (5%). Among other crew members, as many as 17% cited pressure as a cause. In contrast to the officers, bullying (7%; officers: 2%) was also cited, along with disturbed relationships (10%) and loneliness (8%). And here, too, 8% of the respondents referred to insufficient teamwork.

According to Grech et al. there are therefore two concepts, the "authority gradient" and the "leadership style", which must be considered in the perception of the occupation as a group.[54] Since the approach is similar to that of this book, it will now be discussed in more detail. According to the authors, the authority gradient is generally flat or rising, depending on the shape of the relationship and the resulting communication. The following is stated for the hierarchical relationship described above between those of higher rank and those of lower rank: "The authority gradient is the result of the combination of the authority of the captain/officer and the assertiveness of the mate or crew. The authority of the captain could be high and the assertiveness of the crew low. This would make the authority gradient steep. If a high authority is matched by a high assertiveness the authority gradient will appear flatter."[55] In most cases, there is a tense climate on board, so the gradient is steep, as described by Grech et al. This poses the danger that superiors will not be made aware of their mistakes.[56] However, cultural differences should not be neglected in this consideration; people who have been socialised in a strongly authoritative environment, for example, wisely and subconsciously support a rising gradient of authority in maritime working life.[57] "Leadership style and communication are important in relation to authority gradient", the authors continue. However, they do not subscribe to a fatalistic view: "Even though a high formal authority gradient is present, appropriate leadership style and communication can reduce the slope of the gradient."[58] The leadership style and the associated way of conducting conversations are thus seen as making a considerable contribution to a pleasant working and living environment. But the effects on ship safety are also enormous, according to Grech et al. [59] The leadership styles they discuss are listed below.

Interim Conclusion: The Human Factor

At this point, it is appropriate to place the problems described above, which contribute to a psychologically stressful working and living environment, in a broader framework. As this paper largely excludes physical circumstances (nutrition, work, vibration, noise, etc.), the considerations focus on people as social beings, in short, on the human factor in the ship as an organisational unit.

The importance of the human factor for ship operation is considerable, despite all efforts at mechanisation. This *human factor* should not be confused with "human factors" (or in European terms: ergonomics), a science that Grech and others apply to seafaring in order to examine "the notion of fit between the person(s) and their surrounding environment".[60] Thus, the employee is regarded as a human being with needs that are not limited to private life or need to be satisfied only there. "Hence, underlying the subject is the idea that using human factors data, principles, and methods will lead to better designed jobs, tasks, products, or work systems. This in turn will have benefits, both for individuals (through improved well-being) and employers (through improving work performance of individuals and groups in an organisation)",[61] the authors continue. The ITF also complains that there is currently no systematic collection of such relevant data concerning people.[62] Nevertheless, it is also possible for Grech and others to derive concrete measures for action from numerous smaller studies.

The "Human Factors and Ergonomics"[63] are strongly connected to the topic of "Decent Work", which can be traced back to Eva Senghaas-Knobloch. The sociologist of labour discusses the question of human dignity in the world of work against the background of striking differences between the global North and the global South, but also with a view to the international protagonists (including the International Labour Organization (ILO)) of the global labour market.[64] Senghaas-Knobloch attributes a special, albeit not praiseworthy, role to maritime shipping; she also points to the divergence between ownership and operation of ships, i.e. the disappearance of classic shipping companies, and a completely globalised labour market.[65] This results in a noticeable discrepancy: "The current situation in which part of the rules applying to the crew on board are equally valid for all, but another part, especially that for wages and social protection, depends on the nationality of the crew members, makes ships a special place in terms of regulatory policy".[66] Heide Gerstenberger goes on to complain that the lack of opportunity for workers' representation and the resulting disempowerment of the individual and the collective are contrary to the demands of Decent Work.[67] The ITF, Gerstenberger and Senghaas-Knobloch agree, has no really powerful instruments in its hands, at least for the travelling staff.[68]

And so, the human factor dominates the discussion primarily as a source of error; the majority of maritime accidents are attributable to the *human factor*, according to Schellbach.[69] The authors around Michelle Grech, however, plead for a reformed reading and cite considerations by the Swedish scientist Sidney Dekker: "Human error is not a cause of failure. It is the effect, or symptom, of deeper trouble. [...] Human error is not random. It is systematically connected to features of people's tools, tasks, and operating environment. [...] Human error is not the conclusion of an investigation. It is the starting point."[70]

For maritime shipping in particular, this is an almost revolutionary approach that is sure to meet with resistance because it requires explanatory patterns beyond the sole responsibility of the crew and/or the captain. Excluding maliciousness, many of the maritime accidents are due to lack of concentration, fatigue, drunkenness, or simply cognitive overload. In view of the fact that many existing guidelines are hardly observed and monitored, Gerstenberger dampens hopes that the maritime world will change its mindset in favour of "Decent Work".[71] Concrete measures should contribute to a rethinking of the shipping industry.

Business Management Approaches

The presentation and discussion of two proposals in chapter four that could make on-board life satisfactory for all stakeholders must first be placed on a theoretical ground. In the following, therefore, some operational economic approaches will be pursued that primarily concern the area of human resources. Some have already been discussed in research - at least superficially - for maritime shipping or for similarly all-encompassing areas of life and work (for example space travel). Others are taken from classical business or organisational theories and are to be made prolific here for the objective of this work. In doing so, one crux of theoretical, academic reappraisal must not be completely disregarded, which not only the management theorist Nancy J. Adler problematises.[72] Many of the theories applied in the following are tailored to people who were socialised in the so-called global North. In view of the diversity on board seagoing ships, which is also to be mentioned, it goes without saying that people with the most diverse social and cultural backgrounds come together here. Here, too, there is a blind spot that science should at least address, if not eliminate.

Despite these methodological shortcuts, the next step is to look at the crew as a diverse group on the one hand and as a team on the other. This is followed by an in-depth examination of leadership concepts, so that alternative to the strict hierarchy can be identified, which (as sufficiently explained above) can bring problems with it. These three approaches (diversity, team, leadership) will be brought together in this chapter by focusing them on work satisfaction as the highest premise for healthy living (together).

Diversity Management

Diversity in connection with employers often stands for a progressive company, for multicultural coexistence, for needs-based working time models. However, dealing with diversity is not only effective in advertising.[73] In the author's opinion, there is no way around a constructive approach to particularity, especially in highly global working environments such as maritime shipping. Diversity has demonstrable potential and must be channelled in order to have a positive impact on the performance of an organisation, says researcher Doris Gutting.[74] For this reason, organisational theorist Edeltraud Hanappi-Egger and social scientist and economist Roswitha Hofmann describe awareness of heterogeneity as fundamental for organisational and individual diversity competences. This is the only way to recognise the need for action above all and to develop measures.[75] Many organisations lack a corporate culture that welcomes inclusion and thus proactively promotes diversity-sensitive learning.[76]

Successful diversity management is about integrating people with their individual and diverse abilities into an organisation in such a way that they can also contribute in the best possible way to the company.[77] According to Manfred Becker, both the concepts of managing diversity and diversity management are part of this.[78] The economist makes a fundamental distinction between these two aspects: managing diversity means not only recognising the characteristics of an individual or a group of people ("SoSein", English: "being like this"), but also defending them.[79] The focus of action is on eliminating any disadvantages.[80] This is the starting point for diversity management, which favours personal development and proclamation of diversity as a decisive corporate goal.[81] Diversity management is therefore more widespread in the literature. In addition to intercultural management, this term is applied specifically to the maritime sector in the work of Annika Schellbach, which has already been mentioned above.[82] The author criticises the tendency of the industry to view diversity management (DiM) primarily as a cost factor and sees the benefits of a concept tailored to maritime conditions as outweighing the disadvantages.[83]

Diversity must be taken into account, especially when assembling groups such as seafarers who work and live under extreme conditions. The organisational psychologists William B. Vessey and Lauren B. Landon distinguish between two levels: "Surface-level characteristics are readily observable from physical traits (e.g., gender, age, race) or estimated from a few interactions (e.g., occupation, experience, nationality), while deep-level characteristics include values, personality traits, attitudes, and are unobservable."[84] According to this, the superficial characteristics, primarily cultural identity and age on board, recede into the background with constant use and increased stress levels, while it is above all the individual treasures of experience and knowledge that emanate a unifying and productive force.

On board, there is a highly pluralistic staff situation, yet it seems (as shown above) that it has not yet been possible to exploit the advantages of diversity. This is primarily due to the lack of diversity management tools; in onshore work areas, for example, awareness training or programmes to improve the work life balance are such tools.[85] Regular "diversity awareness training" for managers supervised by external companies[86] could also make the personnel implementation of diversity management in the company structure superfluous, which would take into account the special nature of shipping. Heterogeneity channelled in this way can bring positive changes[87] by constructively countering the cumbersome nature of hierarchies in general[88] and communication on merchant ships that is complicated by language diversity.

Diversity must always be kept in mind for the whole organisation. But especially with smaller units, with groups and teams, the smallest complications can endanger an entire project. Therefore, the crew should now be considered as a team. "Cultural diversity provides the greatest potential benefit to teams with challenging tasks that require creativity and innovation", Adler explains. "Diversity becomes less helpful when team members work on simpler tasks involving repetitive or routine procedures."[89] So the more complex the work environment, the more impact diversity can have. The workload in maritime shipping is being distributed on fewer and fewer shoulders, and at the same time the degree of complexity is increasing due to technical innovations - for a long time now, employment on board has been more than just a back-breaking job. In view of this, particular interests and competences must not be neglected in further considerations.

Team

A group of working people is not automatically a team, as the economist and social scientist Anett Hermann also makes clear: "Teams are characterised [...] by self-determined cooperation and a correspondingly large scope for action. [...] In teams, people work together who are strongly task-related, who are characterised by continuous interaction, cooperation and conscious handling of conflicts, and who pursue a common goal. Equality and trust are a prerequisite for this."[90] Teams are therefore a means of organising work, the positive development of which contributes significantly to the success of a company.[91]

Hermann distinguishes the team, defined in detail above, from work groups, a unit of people working together on a task.[92] As the degree of participation and cooperation increases and autonomy grows, working groups could grow into teams.[93] Large parts of the activities on seagoing vessels can be assigned to the most rudimentary, since inevitable, form of group work according to Hermann. Such situations are characterised by collaborative activity without fundamental say or decisive participation.[94] There is no question that a mooring manoeuvre, for example, can only be successful with the help of many crew members from different departments. Here, well-coordinated cooperation is elementary.

However, this type of group work always reaches its limits when crises occur, when individual group members drop out, when routines fail, when - as Adler explains above - innovative and spontaneous action is required. The step towards developing a crew into a team provides a remedy.

First, the socio-psychological concept of group performance will be introduced. A distinction is made between actual and potential group performance (also: group potential), so that a difference becomes apparent between the work result as a group and in the case when each person would have worked independently and individually instead.[95] The group potential in turn depends on the type of task which the business psychologists Felix C. Brodbeck and Stefan Schulz-Hardt divide into additive (the sum of all individual performances), disjunctive (a group-internal negotiation and decision) and conjunctive (a collective cooperation).[96] Brodbeck and Schulz-Hardt cite brainstorming as an example of additive tasks, but the description as adding up all individual performances can be transferred well to everyday professional cooperation on board; especially the strict demarcation between the work areas engine and bridge, which was proble-matised at the beginning, makes it clear that here individuals contribute to the operation of the ship. Since the challenges change according to the situation, seafarers also have to face conjunctive tasks - here, success is only achieved if everyone works equally well and also cooperatively. It is already clear here that the members of a successful team must not only be professionally qualified according to the requirements, but also socially qualified. Moreover, individuals who suffer from untreated mental or physical illnesses are essentially a weak link in the chain of the group. This has a corresponding effect on the group's potential. When putting together teams, even under extreme conditions, too much attention is paid to the professional qualifications of the future colleagues: "The science of composing a team has often fallen victim to composition driven by the intuition of the composers, the technical needs of the mission, or the assumption that anyone can get along for a couple of weeks".[97] Thus, even the cornerstone of team development can cause problems. Hermann refers to the team development model according to

Tuckman/Jensen and puts the composition of the team ("Teamdesign") before the five phases worked out there. Up to now, those responsible have primarily considered professional competences and life circumstances, so that some groups of people (such as single parents) automatically have no chance.[98] Nevertheless, once a team has been put together, it does not remain in its initial state, but continues to develop through a learning curve, among other things. So, there are five phases.[99]

- Forming: Goals, rules and the internal organisation are defined.
- Storming: Social roles are negotiated.
- Norming: Group norms (including communication rules) emerge.
- Performing: The content work is strengthened.
- Adjourning: The project comes to an end with an evaluation.

Particularly in the norming phase, teams show tendencies that demand a certain assimilation of the individual and create homogenisation.[100] Here, as in the composition of the team, another *predetermined breaking point* arises, which reveals itself at the latest in the adjourning phase in the form of criticism and open conflicts. Hermann cautions against chalking up the successful completion of a team's activities as successful group work from an operational point of view. The individual perception of the individual members can deviate greatly from this and in the worst-case lead to inner resignation and ongoing conflicts.[101] Transferred to maritime shipping, this means that an economically well-managed ship without extraordinary incidents of damage does not always indicate a high level of job satisfaction and a well-functioning crew. The internal controversies due to a lack of understanding as a team, which affect mental health and thus also result in staff absenteeism, should therefore not be neglected from the employer's point of view.

The same applies as was said in the previous chapter about diversity; a widespread sensitivity to the problems and opportunities of working in a team is needed. Brodbeck and Schulz-Hardt recommend a multi-perspective awareness that places one's own activity in the context of a joint effort and thus underlines the importance of one's own success for the collective. Investing in measures to create team awareness pays off in the medium term, according to both psychologists.[102] In the composition of crews, their own character as "multicultural teams" must always be kept in mind. Compared to relatively homogeneous groups, members of highly diversified teams are confronted with more challenges, especially when it comes to communication, says Adler. In addition, cohesion within the group, "the ability of team members to act as one", is achieved only slowly and less sustainably in these teams.[103] Nevertheless, the economist sees both advantages and disadvantages,[104] which can also be transferred to an international crew. On the one hand, culturally diverse teams could draw on greater knowledge potential and thus increase the quality and quantity of ideas and options for action.[105] This could lead to better solutions and decisions.[106] On the other hand, the difficulty of communication remains, which contributes to misunderstandings and the loss of important information.[107] Adler also points to increased pressure and stress "primarily due to communication inaccuracies and a lack of trust."[108]

The pitfalls of highly diverse teams are thus quite considerable. Adler therefore complains that although these groups have the greatest potential in an enterprise, this is rarely reflected in reality.[109] This almost serves as a warning for dealing with crews (both on land and on board): "The productivity of a team does not depend on the presence or absence of diversity, but rather on how well diversity is managed."[110] Leaving international crews to their own devices and placing high economic expectations on them at the same time, trusting in their functioning, could therefore almost be described as naïve. There will be no way back to teams that are recruited exclusively from one cultural area, and Adler's considerations do not speak for such homogeneous teams either. Therefore, the levers mentioned in this chapter should be used, as the studies at the beginning show that a lack of togetherness can have severe consequences on the psyche. Those entrusted with crewing should not only pay attention to the availability of personnel who are suitably qualified on paper for the vacant position on board. Already at this stage, when setting up the team, social competences and possibly previous good experience in certain personnel constellations should be considered. Linguistic and intercultural competences should also be assessed (but also trained) and taken into account in personnel decisions.

On arrival on board, however, the direct influence of shore-based personnel policy ends (for the time being). Upon entering the microcosm of the ship, the new crew member is above all subject to the decisions of their superior. As already pointed out by Adler, Hermann also emphasises how important team leadership is for a positive and thus value-creating development of groups: "This includes feedback processes, a clearly defined error culture, transparent information flows, regular review processes and opportunities for co-determination. Only in this way can learning processes and continuous improvements be initiated." This transparency and continuous revision in turn fostered an understanding of the team as an organisational unit.[111]

Leadership is therefore also important in the smallest unit of a large organisation. Before the two concrete measures are presented below, a focussed view on leadership models that have the potential to replace or at least soften the hierarchical structure needs to be taken.

Leadership Approaches

The strict hierarchy on board is hardly questioned. On the one hand, a diffuse sense of tradition dominates, at least among European employees, which is also used as a justification to cover up irregularities ("What happens on board, stays on board.") and is also the reason for the scepticism about trade union work. On the other hand, a hierarchical chain of command is seen as the only efficient one for the manifold tasks. However, this again ignores the fact that on a merchant ship people of different origins and ages come together, who also bring with them very diverse ideas of leadership, power and responsibility. In an international survey in 2007, for example, only 26% of German respondents but 70% of Chinese respondents agreed that hierarchies provided a reassuring knowledge of superiors and their authority. The majority of the Americans interviewed, on the other hand, saw the benefit of hierarchical orders primarily in the distribution of tasks.[112] Moreover, people of different cultural origins perceived their relationship to superiors differently. According to Adler, people from the Philippines are used to a "high power distance", to which a high degree of loyalty but also subordination to patriarchal superiors is linked.[113] For most European people, on the other hand, Adler attributes a "low power-distance"; that is, superiors are valued above all for their expertise and not just for their position in an organisation.[114]

This shows that the hierarchy as the only recognised structure on board can be questioned. So far, in the already limited scientific debate, it has only been discussed in connection with Bridge Team Management (BTM), i.e., with regard to communication between nautical officers and the captain during a manoeuvre. It should be encouraged to extend the considerations on BTM, which are currently being made under the editorship of Jürgen Neff, to the crew as a team.

In the following, three modern business management and leadership concepts are included in order to derive approaches that could be adapted for maritime shipping and conducive to an appreciative living and working environment on merchant ships.

Transformational Leadership

As mentioned above, there is a lack of relevant work on leadership on board; most of the hypotheses and leadership theories presented so far are tailored to a laboratory situation. Therefore, Landon and Vessey criticise: "The majority of leadership research considers there to be a distinct split between leaders and followers [...], a situation that often does not hold true for extreme teams."[115] In extreme situations such as on board, 24/7 availability is usually required, privacy is severely restricted, and the separation between professional and private social environments is almost obsolete.

Therefore, according to the two organisational psychologists, such groups tend to have "more informal leadership structures with multiple individuals fulfilling leadership roles as the situation and work demands."[116] The hierarchies originally established in these teams are often consciously and even unknowingly broken through, which, however, profitably contributes to cohesion and flexibility of action.[117] Leadership can therefore be viewed in two ways: "Leadership as a role is bound to a person who thus exercises the leadership role. In contrast, leadership as a social process is characterised by several people, so that no clear assignment of roles is possible".[118] The social meaning of leadership is thus also a permanent and above all internal negotiation process.

With transactional and transformational leadership, two leadership styles are currently being discussed in research that initially seem to be at odds with each other. The *transactional* leadership style (work for money, duty fulfilment for praise, failure to achieve goals for reprimand) focuses primarily on extrinsic motivation of employees.[119] The author Olaf Kortmann sees transactional leaders as managers who act and decide according to the requirements of the tasks, but lose sight of the people and their needs.[120] Moreover, this conventional way of guiding people has reached its limits, as the impersonal relationship between supervisors and employees is not up to date. Moreover, intrinsic motivation remains unused.[121] Even more, transactional leadership is an "Anleitung zur Mittelmäßigkeit" (English: guide to mediocrity), according to Justus Jeromin.[122]

Transformational leadership aims to shape, i.e., transform, not only the behaviour, but also the attitude of the employees and the leader.[123] It does not rely on monetary reward systems that are not very sustainable, but on the effect of a role model.[124] In contrast to maintaining familiar structures, this style of leadership demands a change in behaviour from superiors. The economist Waldemar Pelz suggests achieving the greatest possible intersection with the following statements:

- "He (or she) means what he says"
- "Stands for clear values"
- "Set clear goals and expectations"
- "Has profound expertise" ("breadth" vs. "depth")
- "Is open to criticism and new ideas"
- "He/she can be relied upon"
- "Behaves in a manner that commands respect"[125]

Following these guiding principles also has a positive effect on the manager, since unlike in a transactional management relationship, the manager benefits from the improved personal, less stressful relationships.[126] Kortmann also sees this style of leadership as a challenge for the manager, as they should hand over responsibility with a clear conscience and encourage the employees to work independently.[127] At the same time, they should constantly question themselves, amend their own behaviour[128] and avoid the danger of falling into a self-aggrandisement.[129]

Two aspects are particularly important regarding the above-mentioned topic. On the one hand, a change from transactional to transformational leadership takes time. Kortmann warns, for example, that employees can initially be overwhelmed by the newly acquired personal responsibility.[130] On the other hand, a transformational way of leading has a positive effect on the health of employees; the all-embracing view of work and the working environment, but also the increased social component could contribute to a pleasant situation.[131]

According to Beate Mödler, interpersonal relationships, both between superiors and employees and among colleagues, are an important economic factor and yet are often neglected in reality: "Working relationships seem so self-evident that they are usually only noticed when conflicts arise." Or when the unhappiness is reflected in a corresponding level of sick leave.[132] Mödler further criticises the fact that leadership tasks are often only perceived as content-related work.[133] She therefore suggests a system-sensitive understanding of leadership, which also perceives interaction as an area of responsibility for managers.[134] For example, the responsibility for good communication lies primarily with the leaders, since an increased emotional bond leads to increased motivation to work among the staff.[135] Kortmann suggests a constructive combination of both styles; especially in crisis situations that require a lean structure, transactional leadership may also be necessary, without neglecting fairness and disclosure of goals.[136]

Experience shows that transactional leadership is very strong in the maritime industry. Sometimes people who do not perform one hundred percent as expected, who are criticised or who are prejudiced because of their gender, nationality, or skin colour, may get the impression that they have to fear a subjective and thus negative evaluation by the captain. Depending on the terms of the contract, this could jeopardise re-employment with that shipping company or crewing agency. According to the author's findings, the strained relationship can sometimes lead to a tense atmosphere and a bad mood even during the time on board, with devastating effects on the mental health of those affected. There are also reports of open and loud conflicts. This is where transformational leadership could have a positive effect, in that leaders present themselves as role models not only in the way they work but also in the way they interact.

The majority of activities on board are routine tasks, for which a fair transactional leadership style with a pronounced feedback loop seems sufficient. Beyond that, however, the seafarers' personal responsibility and creative power can be strengthened. According to the author, the path leads through creative problem solving and an open culture of criticism. Up to now, when a seafarer needs to complete a dangerous but unavoidable task, they need to fill out a checklist with safety precautions taken before carrying out the task. This can carry the risk that under stressful conditions some items are less carefully checked and pro forma confirmed. In addition, these checklists are designed exclusively methodically, i.e., primarily with emphasise on tools/equipment and not personal factors such as skill or state of mind prior to performing the dangerous task. There is no potential for new approaches, for the expression of discomfort and security concerns. A standardised checklist may not take into account the mental and physical dualities of the seafarers or the physical characteristics of the ship on which the task needs to be performed. It could be more effective to hold discussions with the supervisors before and after such activities, in which the course of action would be individually determined and subsequently evaluated. Here, transformational leaders could prove to be profitable, as they have the empathy and at the same time radiate a confident, agile attitude.

Shared Leadership and Hierarchy

Up to this point, a combination of transactional and transformational components could be identified as a potentially valuable leadership style in maritime shipping, with the emphasis shifting according to the situation. Each person's own way of leading and being led could be explained. At the beginning, however, the limits of hierarchy as an organisational structure were also pointed out. In the following, the focus will be on the vertical power and responsibility structures on board. In conclusion, an alternative will be discussed briefly.

The author Herbert Happel, on the other hand, pleads *for* hierarchical teams and organisations. First and foremost, hierarchy has an ordering function that structures the position and relationship of people within an organisation.[137] This results in a vertical arrangement that provides a lot of clarity about responsibility, duties and decisions. Interestingly, Happel attributes a great deal of creative capacity to hierarchy, as it gives rise to important creative leeway.[138] The economists Sigrid Endres and Jürgen Weibler, for example, disagree; hierarchies are not considered to be very agile or progressive.[139]

Happel lists a total of nine advantages, which make clear the equally limiting and creative effect of hierarchies.[140] Not all of these can be considered fulfilled in maritime shipping. It is true that hierarchies manifest power structures, some of which can be useful for the goal-oriented accomplishment of a task (advantage 1). In this way, one's own position within an organisation - ergo: a crew - is clearly regulated (advantage 2).[141] Consequently, there is no need to fight over the distribution of power; the recipient and the giver of the command can be detected as far as possible without dispute. And yet, in practice onboard, it shows how difficult it is to formally legitimate the captain's orders in contradiction of the chief engineer's. Decisions made on the bridge regarding workings in the engine room may not always be technically feasible or sensible. This is where the resolution of clear communication, which Happel mentions as the fifth advantage, also fails: "Organisational awareness of one's own place in the hierarchy helps to distinguish between equal discussion, negotiation, consultation on the one hand and instructing, delegating, allowing oneself to be consulted in complementary roles on the other."[142] Not only, but especially Neff et al., deal in depth with the understanding between the bridge crew, which is influenced by many factors. Unfortunately, it is beyond the scope of this book to go into more detail on communication within the ship's hierarchy as a whole - this is where specialist research (also against the background of cultural diversity) can come in.

It is difficult to recognise Happel's fourth and sixth advantages in the organisational unit ship. The author emphasises that hierarchies are fundamentally immanent in a duty of care, from the point of view that employees are indispensable to the success of an organisation (advantage 4).[143] However, the global labour market for maritime personnel is an almost unavailable source of ever cheaper labour. For the reasons mentioned above, workers' interests find little resonance; rather, shipping companies and personnel agency seem to determine not only the monetary conditions but also the working and living conditions. If no personal bond can develop between crew members on board, they quickly get used to ever-changing constellations - the person, the colleague becomes substitutable. What Happel values in terms of "institutioneller Hygiene"[144] (English: institutional hygiene), the working relationship that is more or less free of personal concerns (advantage 6), can inevitably lead to isolation in the sea voyage; after all, the crew is both a colleague and a social environment at the same time.

Against the background of on-board reality, the limits of Happel's approach become clear. The author writes about the recognised dangers of vertical power structures: "However, a continuing unlimited abuse of hierarchy and structure to the detriment of the individual - according to my positive view and confidence - will not last in the long run because of the self-image, the relevance and the survival strategy of the organisation. For then there will be disruptions in the fulfilment of tasks and, via feedback loops, changes towards the survival of the institution, further development and a positive use of hierarchy."[145]

For the reasons that follow, the author takes a critical view of this. In the maritime shipping industry there is a lack of neutral and at the same time powerful complaints bodies, partly due to the lack of workers' associations.[146] Those affected have the impression that from a land-based perspective there is no need to intervene and to discipline or train managers on board as long as a ship runs reasonably without damage and in the best case with few expenses. Furthermore, the fact that regular crews are seldom established and many seafarers are confronted with ever new ships and ever different crews means that there is no need to protect the survival of the (concrete) organisational unit, as Happel calls it, in the long term by providing a good working atmosphere and a field of activity worth living in. Here, people often just drive by sight.

Hierarchy on board is therefore not an uncontroversial concept for several reasons; the conditions of this work environment are too specific. According to Landon and Vessey, leaders who are selected primarily on the basis of their technical expertise, both on board and in other extremely stressful and self-sufficient work environments, must combine diverse leadership models: "[...] Leaders of extreme teams need to be able to engage in multiple types of leadership, including shared leadership, socioemotional leadership when dealing with personal or interpersonal issues within the team, and crisis-response leadership, which is often the one situation in which formal authority is more heavily emphasised in these environments, and which may require a more directive leadership style [...]."[147] The authors describe *shared leadership* as a starting point for situational changes in leadership behaviour, as all team members have comprehensive knowledge of the overall situation and are therefore better able to assess directive decisions.

Endres and Weibler point out that networks, too, do not create individual leaders but form collaborations; the participants thus bring in their own competences.[148] In such groups, the search for consensus is in the foreground, whereby individual expertise, but also the wealth of experience of all is incorporated.[149] Shared leadership is described here as a relatively natural consultation in which classic leadership tasks are divided among several people.[150] Endres and Weibler therefore cite a cluster that brings together, on the one hand, the leadership style (including transactional or trans formational) and the organisational distribution of leadership (vertical leadership or shared leadership). The mandate to recognise errors, i.e. to monitor performance (transactional leadership style) shifts from the team leadership (vertical leadership) to the team members (shared leadership). The same applies to the assumption of transformational leadership, according to which everyone performs at their best.[151]

In a group where leadership is perceived as a collective task, several team members take the place of individual leadership. Leadership is thus a matter of negotiation and social necessity, almost natural.[152] For Endres and Weibler, too, leadership is therefore the result of shared participation, which requires leadership competence on the one hand and the willingness to follow on the other hand.[153] However, the authors also point out that shared leadership is not suitable for standardised or routine fields of activity. Such concepts would only develop their real potential in complex areas where a high density of knowledge would lead to innovative solutions to problems.[154] So were Landon and Vessey wrong when they favoured shared leadership for extreme areas of work?

Shared leadership works when all employees are not the same but are similarly highly qualified and therefore enter into discourse with each other at eye level. This cannot be assumed of the crew team; here, not only different areas of expertise come together, but also people with individual experience values and diverse training. It is not appropriate to make decisions collectively, neither in everyday challenges nor in extraordinary situations. However, this does not mean that the captain has a sole mandate, as the dangers of centralising power in hierarchies have been sufficiently pointed out. It could be useful to involve at least the other "heads of department" in important decisions - and then to communicate the basis for the decision openly to all.

Nautical expert Thomas Jung therefore distinguishes between "boss" and "leader", whereby crews would prefer the latter.[155] According to this, leaders act as coaches who promote the further development of the crew through motivating and exemplary behaviour. These leaders do not place themselves verbally above the group but communicate and act inclusively and trustingly. In contrast, leaders of the Boss type elevate themselves above the crew through their authority and monopoly of knowledge. This is underlined by ego-centred speech. According to Jung, there is also a difference in the way they deal with human failure; while bosses would react to mistakes with censure in an environment that is already characterised by fear, leaders derive constructive changes from them.[156]

"The best leaders are situational leaders. They understand the challenges of a situation, match their style flexibly to people's motives and need for direction, and provide support for achieving the specific goal at that moment."[157] According to Jung, (nautical) leaders should have and develop both directive and supportive leadership skills.[158] At this point it is not possible to present a conclusive statement on an ideal leadership model on board merchant ships - if it is possible at all. Up to this point, however, it can be suggested that leadership be perceived as an important linchpin of shipboard cooperation and that urgent improvements be made at least to the training content of future managers (i.e. in Germany in the course of nautical and ship operation studies). Managers must become aware of their function and their role as "coach or mentor" and adapt their actions accordingly, Jung appeals.[159]

So, it is worthwhile to take another modern approach to shaping leadership.

Feel Good Management

"A group becomes a team when it pursues common goals and missions, communicates actively in an optimal atmosphere and everyone assumes responsibility for this. This can only happen in daily communication, in a lively exchange of all important information as well as active work on a trusting and respectful atmosphere", Neff explains with regard to the bridge team. He takes the captain in particular to task as the "master of atmosphere".[160] But the resolutions that Neff attaches to this position can also be applied to the chief engineer:[161]

- Observation of operational processes (view from outside)
- Observation of the way of dealing
- Embodying a model of behaviour

The captain should always pay special attention to the various forms of communication, i.e.: what is expressed and how is it understood?[162] What is needed is an environment in which superiors not only reprimand, but also encourage criticism; in which criticism is not either ignored or understood as an existential threat to the work place. An environment in which upward criticism is also allowed.

Here, an insight into the so-called Feel Good Management as an approach that inscribes a holistic and sustainable interaction with each other into the corporate culture cannot be omitted. This is how organisations should be able to work more successfully.[163] Organisationally, a Feel Good Manager can be established as a permanent position in a company or its human resources department (HR). However, aspects can also be extracted that can be implemented in the individual management style on board as well; provided that the corporate culture allows it.[164] Feel Good Management does not aim to change working hours in general, but to improve life at work.[165] This assumption of the authors Sophia Gesing and Ulrike Weber encourages to also transfer the approach to maritime shipping, where the 0-4 or 0-6 watch system[166] is currently unchallenged (here, too, alternatives to the very unnatural working and sleeping rhythm could be considered).

According to this, the tasks of a Feel Good Manager would include the establishment or improvement of company team building and onboarding procedures, internal communication as well as health care (including, among other things, ergonomics).[167] The onboarding process in particular is highlighted in the fourth chapter as a significant measure to focus on the arrival of seafarers on the ship.

Feel Good Management keeps employees in the company by promoting their motivation and maintaining their work performance[168] - and could thus also be an effective instrument to prevent mental illnesses due to stress. However, Gesing and Weber point out that a flat hierarchy is a necessary prerequisite.[169] This also applies to the Well-Being Concept, which is more widespread in Anglo-Saxon countries, but which is clearly to be found in HR.[170] This concept has five dimensions, all of which were identified in the above section as problem areas on board. In addition to health and good working conditions, the focus here is on the prospect of individual development, nurturing relationships and good leadership.[171] Aspects of Feel Good Management and Well-Being do not necessarily have to be combined in a newly created position in the company, it is also possible to incorporate them into a "positive management style": "Instead of hierarchical power, there is a need for lateral and participative leadership that strengthens cooperation and trust."[172] A fair management therefore no longer regards employees merely as a resource.[173]

Recommendations for HR Management

In the first part of this book, it was impressively shown that many of the mental illnesses on board, which in the worst-case lead to suicide, have their origin in social isolation. The isolation can be due to the conscious withdrawal of the individual, who has to struggle with homesickness, the language barrier, the pressure of work and the impression of not being properly integrated either in professional life or ashore. However, the previous chapter also shows what influence the relationship between superiors and employees, as well as the collective togetherness has on the well-being of the individual.

The author is only aware of measures taken by individual shipping companies to accompany working life on board. Experience has shown that many seafarers' on-board assignments begin relatively hastily; sometimes the news about the next ship reaches them together with the flight details for the journey a few days before they are due to go on duty. The moment of relief on board is also hectic and usually has to be integrated into the already often tense daily routine in port. In some cases, the person being relieved prepares a written handover in which processing statuses and future tasks are noted down. This is usually not required of staff beyond the technical or nautical officer ranks. At most, they are informed verbally about the tasks, persons, and locations. There is not always time for a technical handover, let alone for a personal arrival.

According to safety regulations (Convention for the Safety of Life at Sea (SOLAS) and/or International Safety Management Code (ISM Code)), regular group meetings and exercises are held during shipboard operations to familiarise all crew members with the safety-relevant facilities and measures on board. From own experience, these (similar to checklists) are often only dealt with pro forma; often there is not enough time, or the numerous regulations lead to habituation. Furthermore, there is a tendency for communal activities, where personal aspects or aspects concerning the environment can be discussed in an informal way, to become more and more scarce. Moreover, the few barbecues or karaoke sing-alongs after work at sea always leave watchkeepers somewhat out in the cold.

A relatively widespread procedure for evaluating social and professional behaviour is the final written employee evaluation, for example in the form of a standardised evaluation form, which is submitted to the crew member (depending on the captain) before being passed on to the crewing agency and/or shipping company. This assessment partly determines whether a crew member will be re-employed or promoted in the hierarchy. Whether there is constructive (!) intervention by superiors during the assignment so that the crew member can change their behaviour and actions accordingly depends, as experience shows, very much on the individual manager.

Leadership style and characteristics can be learned and trained. Likewise, a working environment can be created in which all participants contribute to an appreciative and pleasant atmosphere. In the following, two concrete measures will be presented, which are mainly found in younger companies such as start-ups and are now being adapted in older ones. For active sea shipping, at least individual aspects should be considered and implementation on board held out in prospect.

Onboarding

The onboarding process not only fits the onboarding situation very well in name. A targeted procedure to bring employees into the company helps to achieve "organisationale Sozialisation" (English: organisational socialisation). This means the targeted integration of the individual through the compressed transfer of professional, but also social and normative knowledge, so that new employees quickly find their role within the structure.[174] Seafarers who join a new crew and a new ship also have to find their place. As shown above, the role assigned in the form of a rank is by no means sufficient. The social role must also be formed to give the crew member a positive arrival and a feeling of being valued as a person and as a worker.

The business psychologists around Klaus Moser therefore make a distinction between instruction (German: Einweisung) and onboarding. The German term refers more to the technical familiarisation with new challenges and is also terminated. What is more, onboarding is on the contrary, as just described, more of a process, lasting and thus not limited to a few days.[175] Brenner also attributes a comprehensive effect to this procedure and highlights three levels of integration of new employees. Firstly, professional expertise must be acquired, which means organisational knowledge as well as practical knowledge (professional integration). Secondly, integration into the new social environment is necessary; only then can the new colleague find a social role in the team (social integration). Thirdly, the company's values must be communicated in a sustainable way that does not neglect leadership principles (value-oriented integration).[176]

Moser et al. identify four stressors that affect a new group member: disappointed expectations, uncertainty and feelings of stress resulting from the unfamiliar personnel environment and the new tasks.[177] However, the business psychologists also emphasise that the need for onboarding measures varies from person to person.[178] Therefore, they start with a needs analysis, which explores the organisation, the field of activity and the person to be hired, so that suitable steps can be derived from this.[179]

So-called preboarding precedes the physical arrival at a new company. Here, the focus is not on imparting knowledge but on personal familiarisation and an initial feeling of welcome.[180] Even though onboard assignments are often spontaneous, it is conceivable, for example, to send the new crew members at least some data (about the ship, the crew, the voyage route) and words of welcome on board by e-mail. In this way, the future supervisors would also get to know the person arriving and based on this, could provide the rest of the crew with information about the next colleague.

The first day of work should be well planned, the new workplace set up and the staff well informed as part of sustainable onboarding.[181] A poorly prepared team, according to Brenner, suggests unprofessionalism and leaves newcomers feeling unappreciated.[182] This is a good approach for maritime shipping, where respect for the individual, as shown, sometimes clearly falls by the wayside. The shipping companies and/or personnel agencies could provide the captains with some personnel information for further dissemination. In addition, it is small gestures that should be well prepared: the reliable checking of the chamber to be occupied, the provision of fresh bed linen, drinks and protective clothing before the arrival of the relief. It is also a matter of concern, given the stress of the voyage, that many seafarers have to start work immediately on arrival and replace their predecessor. So, there is little time to settle in or settle down, so some preparations could already be made here. A short greeting of new crew members by the captain and the responsible supervisor should also be established as a standard procedure upon arrival.

Furthermore, target agreements and feedback discussions can be part of a balanced and long-term onboarding process.[183] Some of the many ways in which onboarding can be organised will be discussed in the next subsection. Here, transferability to the onboarding situation is conceivable, although probably not on the first day of work. Brenner also suggests a mentorship between a colleague and the new employee; not only could professional knowledge be passed on, but a contact person would also be created in addition to the previous manager.[184] It is quite conceivable to create such a position as a trusted person on board as well, although the unequal length of the contracts makes it difficult to entrust such tasks in the long term.

Onboarding can thus be a valuable tool to integrate seafarers into the new working and living environment and to lay the foundation for a fully-fledged participating crew member. However, it is also clear that this procedure brings together diverse measures and methods from different contexts.[185] They are initially designed for office work and not all of them are suitable for active maritime navigation. Nevertheless, the idea of proactively shaping the working relationship is again central here. The literature to date can provide inspiration for creating a working environment for seafarers that feels as much like a valuable living environment as possible and at the same time supports the idea of teamwork.

Staff Appraisal

The organisational psychologist Oswald Neuberger refers to the astonishing result of a study that highlights a direct connection between internal communication and group performance. According to this study, group performance increases when superiors also add an individual and personal component to the working relationship.[186] Informal discussions can therefore lead to a pleasant working atmosphere and thus be an integral part of management based on Feel Good Management. Employee interviews are a personnel management instrument for regulating professional communication. Mentzel et al. clarify: "Employee appraisals include all conversations between superiors and their employees that go beyond routine everyday communication. [...] Staff appraisals are management tasks and therefore cannot be delegated."[187] In contrast to the psychologist Urs Alter, who sees both employees and supervisors as having a duty,[188] the authors see the employee interview as a (often neglected) task of managers.[189]

"The appraisal interview is a purpose interview conducted with a very specific intention."[190] This intention can be recurring or also triggered by something. There are different categorisations, but Mentzel et al. distinguish three types of discussions. Regular appraisal interviews are, for example, target agreement interviews, appraisal interviews and promotion interviews.[191] Sometimes, however, situational discussions are necessary, for example, for introduction, disciplining or in case of conflicts. In exceptional cases, the authors also include team discussions, which leave behind the characteristic of an individual discussion.[192] Such moderated group conferences are a charming idea, also in maritime shipping, where there are otherwise few moments when the crew can constitute itself as a team under regulated conditions. For this to happen, however, the framework conditions would first have to be adapted, as facilitation requires good planning and, above all, methodological skills.[193] So here too, not all types of discussions are equally suitable for maritime shipping. So far, the author is only aware of the large Danish logistics company Maersk holding regular talks on board - unfortunately, the contact persons did not respond to enquiries. With a view to the cycle of an assignment, three potent possibilities should therefore be considered: The induction interview, the departure interview, and an assessment interview in between. In addition to this, an upward and downward assessment should be discussed.

Introductory and Final Discussion

Following on from the above considerations on onboarding, the author considers an introductory talk to be useful. According to the authors around Mentzel, the focus here is on getting to know each other. It is an opportunity for the employee to formulate their own expectations of the new professional challenges, the supervisor and the colleagues. Conversely, the manager can express initial goals at this point and make them more concrete in terms of time. Moreover, the position within the working group can also be explained.[194] Such a discussion at the beginning of a board assignment could prevent misunderstandings on both sides and contribute to an appreciative relationship. Concrete target agreements, which have no adequate equivalent due to the recurring activities on board, could be replaced by the expressed expectations of the working method. At this point it would become clear in the conversation what leadership characteristics the crew member has to deal with; how much consultation does the supervisor require, who controls the work, how much room is there for independence?

The onboard assignment could therefore be framed by an entry interview and an exit interview. The so-called "Abgangsgespräch" (English: exit interview) is foreseen by Mentzel, among others, when an employee leaves the company after termination; different, then, from the foreseen situation on board, when seafarers leave the ship after the expiry of their assignment contract. But here too, expertise and experience are lost each time.[195] A final interview, which no longer affects the assessment, can therefore provide valuable, subjective information about the working atmosphere and circumstances on the ship. Mentzel et al. suggest a record sheet that can be given to the interviewer as a guide. This can be used to find out how the crew member perceived their own area of responsibility, but also the behaviour of the leadership and the working conditions.[196] If it is possible to create a relaxed atmosphere for the discussion, the supervisor can derive measures for them. In addition, the shipping company or personnel agency could draw conclusions from the results about the leadership strengths and weaknesses, but also about the crew member's compatibility with the team. A corresponding personnel policy would make it possible to deploy seafarers in a more targeted manner on this basis and to avoid conflictual constellations.

Both the entry and exit interviews are not particularly planning intensive, do not take much time and yet, in the author's opinion, have an enormous effect on self-image. It is suggested to the crew members that they are more than just a replacement for the predecessor in the position to be held and that their knowledge is also important after leaving the ship. Thus, the establishment of such debates is an important contribution to an appreciative relationship with a other and contributes to a dignified image of humanity.

Appraisal Interview

Both the feedback discussion and the appraisal discussion have qualities that would justify their inclusion in the maritime discussion canon: "In terms of content, the appraisal discussion has a lot in common with the feedback discussion. In both cases, it is about recognising good performance and improving poor performance. [...] While the feedback interview is a snapshot, the appraisal interview unfolds far-reaching - consequences."[197] Since assessment sheets have found their way into maritime shipping anyway, a connection can certainly be sought here. Two assessment systems come into question. In many areas, it is above all the employee appraisals that have prevailed (downwards), but an upwards appraisal is also conceivable, i.e., information from the employees about the leadership behaviour and working methods of their superiors. In view of the above-mentioned problematic leadership situation on board, both possibilities should be examined.

Both parties are under pressure to justify their performance in appraisal interviews. Here, the discrepancy between external and self-perception often comes to light.[198] The more precisely the manager has made their own expectations clear, for example during the initial interview, the smaller the discrepancy. However, it remains a situation in which praise is accompanied by reprimands.

Neuberger speaks of four aspects in recognition and criticism alike:

- Information aspect, i.e., valid and factual evidence for a deviation from the norm (upwards or downwards) is provided.[199]
- Learning aspect, i.e., behaviour is to be maintained or discarded.[200]
- Motivational aspect, i.e., employees felt either rewarded or punished by words of praise or criticism.[201]
- Social aspect, i.e., effects on social behaviour are to be measured.[202]

The latter aspect in particular makes it clear how much sensitivity is needed when voicing complaints - even more so in isolation on board than in working relationships on land. Neuberger therefore points to the threat to the self-image posed by critical feedback, but also to the impairment of the personal relationship between the critic and the criticised.[203] Particularly in the case of pronounced hierarchies, the immanent power distance can increase further: "Criticism then develops into a routine ritual in which the employee demonstrates their submission and gets away with it once again without anything changing in the long run. Recognition and criticism are then seen as a means of marking and conserving the existing hierarchical distances."[204]

Neuberger thus unconsciously draws attention to a problem (not only) in maritime shipping. Partly loud and emotional criticism often seems to result from a lack of other outlets, one's own frustration and lack of methodological skills (speechlessness). Subordinate crew members react to this with gestures of humility, e.g., fear of getting fired, and are equally unable to express their feelings of unfair treatment. In such cases, criticism presented in an unprofessional manner can lead to emotions that are passed on from top to bottom through the crew - or, in the worst case, trigger massive mental crises in the individual.

Accordingly, certain behavioural patterns are indicated for appraisal interviews, which, according to Neuberger, differ between critical and praising statements. On the one hand, it is important to differentiate between positive comments, as not everything is equally praiseworthy, on the other hand, routine activities can also be honourable.[205] In addition, it is essential to be binding, especially in appreciative talks; praise alone only satisfies employees in the short term.[206] Within the framework of an onboard appraisal discussion, binding agreements on the next assignment (promotion, return to the same ship or to a preferred assignment area) could be the result. But this requires a corresponding willingness on the part of the crew to follow the ship's recommendations. For critical discussions, Neuberger recommends first establishing a positive contact and signalling a constructive attitude.[207] Here, too, the appraisal conversation on board may have laid the first useful foundation. In addition, Neuberger continues, the supervisor should not be led by rumours and should avoid generalisations.[208] Objective criticism can only bear fruit if such a discussion ends on a positive note.[209] Threats, for example, that otherwise one's employment would be endangered, do not correspond to this and do not usually lead to a lasting change in behaviour.

If these behavioural norms are taken into account, an oral upward appraisal would also be quite conceivable. So far, this instrument is often known in written form.[210] However, Cyrus Achouri points out that an anonymous, non-verbal assessment by superiors turns out worse than an openly expressed one. He therefore pleads for a situation conducive to conversation, for example in team fostering workshops, where an intimate and at the same time anonymous setting can be created.[211] Such comprehensive measures are difficult to transfer to the crew of a merchant ship, which, moreover, is always being put together a new. Digital supervision sessions could be considered here if the technical conditions allow.

However, the advantages of supervisor appraisals cannot be minimised. Companies have to measure their own understanding of leadership against this, Achouri explains, and it also provides an indicator of the working atmosphere. Last but not least, employees also benefit directly from this tool, which creates a sense of responsibility and gives them a mandate to actively shape their relationship with their superiors.[212] For organisational psychologist Friedemann Nerdinger, upward appraisal therefore has an important participatory function; a strengthened relationship between employees and managers increases satisfaction and inevitably improves work results.[213] In addition to the two well-known models (as an anonymous questionnaire or in the course of a workshop)[214], Nerdinger also mentions "wechselseitige Rückmeldegespräche" (English: mutual feedback discussions), which are organised as individual or group discussions. Formalisation is not possible here, which also makes comparability difficult.[215] This could be a time-saving solution for maritime shipping, but it could fail due to the inexperience with such interview situations and the often-tense conditions. Therefore, written assessments of all supervisors, not just the captain, would probably be the most practical means.

A supervisor appraisal, regardless of format, would give all crew members a new sense of self-worth and counteract the impression of being voiceless and powerless. It would certainly take some time from introduction to establishment, i.e., until there are meaningful results at the end. It must be clearly communicated that the assessors are not threatened with any consequences. At the same time, this instrument can only be effective if employers do not draw hasty conclusions from the assessments. For fear of the consequences of unobjective judgements, superiors on board would certainly allow fewer opportunities for such assessment measures. At this point, clear reference must be made to the constructive aspects of praise and reprimand and development time must be allowed.

In order to follow the narrow path between transactional and transformational leadership in the maritime environment, forms of conversational leadership are therefore certainly suitable. In this way, managers on board could receive feedback independent of the shipping company, evaluate their actions internally and, if necessary, realign them. At the same time, the other seafarers experience appreciation through the discussion options presented here, in that they are given a voice and are shown development perspectives.

Who will answer the call?

The previous pages have highlighted a far-reaching problem in an environment that no longer has anything to do with seafaring romance and yet should concern all consumers. Maritime shipping poses an enormous health risk to seafarers, which is why in the past measures were mainly introduced to improve the physical living conditions (individual chambers, leisure facilities). The causes and significance of mental illness for the individual, on the other hand, have so far been little addressed.

The unusual constellation of an almost isolated, often exclusively male community leads to a far-reaching speechlessness and even a taboo against even discussing emotional concerns and, in serious cases, mental suffering. There is a lack of safe spaces and trustworthy, medically well-trained contact persons who could recognise signals of serious mental illnesses at an early stage. Clear alarm signs such as alcohol abuse and apathy are often ignored in such an environment.

The entity ship remains a very complex field of study influenced by many factors: "Seafaring has long combined paradoxes, such as social exclusion and continuous social proximity, confinement in open spaces, and multiculturalism, within the single organisational culture of a ship. Consistencies - such as social isolation and confinement with shipmates - are evident in onboard working and living condition [...]."[216] Further empirical studies are needed not only to recognise the problem of mental illness (with suicidal consequences) but also to evaluate psychological countermeasures. In this way, an awareness of the problem could be created in the maritime industry.

This book has made some initial suggestions on how the social structure on board can be reformed to create an appreciative climate. Without the willingness of the shipping companies and/or the personnel agencies, this will not be fully possible. There is no doubt that the subsequent training of seafarers in leadership positions involves costs. However, should the expected effects occur in the medium term, i.e., the mental health of the individuals on board improves, the number of serious cases resulting in death should also be reduced. This could also reduce the number of absences due to illnesses and accidents, which would significantly decrease unscheduled crew changes or interruptions to the itinerary.

Furthermore, the universities (in Germany; the training of seafarers is only little regulated internationally by the International Convention on Standards of Training, Certification and Watchkeeping for Seafarers (STCW)) are called upon to focus more on mental health care and organisational psychology. Only when prospective seafarers, especially those with the prospect of a personnel responsibility, understand the organisational context, can a comprehensive understanding of leadership be derived from it. Responsibility for the ship must more clearly imply a sense of duty towards the physical and spiritual well-being of the crew.

When presenting the problems in the first part of the book, reference could also be made to the lack of digital infrastructure on board many seagoing vessels and the resulting increased isolation of seafarers. Investing in stable networks that are accessible to all could not only serve to entertain and keep in touch with individuals. It could also be used for training by external trainers, for example in the sense of supervision. Of course, appropriate offers would first have to be developed that take into account the time capacities on board and the distance.

Within the framework of appropriate training or further education, the measures discussed, i.e., onboarding and a variety of discussion routines, can gradually find their way into active maritime shipping. Without a doubt, the introduction of such initial moments by the shipping company, for example, will initially be met with resistance on board, as many seafarers already feel unduly burdened by new tasks and in combination with reduced number of crew members. Here, those responsible on shore have to promote the means with a certain tact. A clumsy regulation, which where possible is in turn subject to disciplinary consequences for non-compliance, would only lead to a further undermining of what is actually a sensible provision. Maritime shipping certainly does not need another checklist that is checked off pro forma and filed away.

This work is therefore to be understood as a stimulus to an interdisciplinary discussion that uses the merchant ship as an extreme example of a globalised world of work. In view of the massive encroachment of maritime employment on the self-determination of individuals, action is urgently needed to further protect the seafarers' integrity. It will not be possible to fundamentally change the maritime world, which has been globalised down to the smallest detail. This makes it all the more urgent to focus on the smallest unit, the ship and its crew:

"The operation of shipping development requires human devotion. In this case, the quality and quantity of seafarers, the basis of a merchant ship, is getting emphasized."[217]

[1]   Kruecken,   Stefan   (2020):   SOS   an   Heiligabend,   online: https://www.spiegel.de/karriere/seeleute-in-der-corona-krise-s-o-s-an-heiligabend-a-195be52b-0634-460b-aa7f-46231a6353a7.

[2] Kruecken (2020).

[3]   Lützhöft/Styhr/Petersen/Abeysiriwardhane: The   Psychology   of   Ship Architecture and Design, in: MacLachlan, Malcom (ed.): Maritime Psychology. Research in Organizational & Health Behavior at Sea, Cham 2017, p. 73.

[4] A mortality study concludes that "the age-stratified accident rate of German seafarers   aboard   [...]   is   12   times   higher   than   mortality   ashore". (Harth/Herzog/Oldenburg: Seafarer deaths at sea: a German mortality study, in: Occupational Medicine, 66/2016, p. 137). A Danish survey also found that the risk of a fatal accident was six times higher than for other workers. (Borch/Burr/Hansen/Jepsen: Surveillance of maritime deaths on board Danish merchant ships, 1986-2009, in: International Maritime Health, 1/2012, p. 7).

[5] ITF: Summary report from the ITF Seafarers' Trust Autumn 2016 workshop on Social Isolation Depression and Suicide (SIDS), op. cit. 2016.

[6] Lefkowitz, Rafael Y./Slade, Martin D.: Seafarer Mental Health Study, London 2019.

[7] MacLachlan (2017).

[8] Grech, Michelle R./Horberry, Tim J./Koester, Thomas: Human factors in the maritime domain, Boca Raton 2008.

[9] Neff, Jürgen (ed.): Improving Bridge Resource Management. Human Factors in Maritime Safety, Leverkusen 2020.

[10] Gerstenberger, Heide: "Decent Work" in der Seeschifffahrt?, in: Becke, Guido/Bleses, Peter/Ritter, Wolfgang/Schmidt, Sandra (eds.): Decent Work. Arbeitspolitische Gestaltungsperspektive für eine globalisierte und flexibilisierte Arbeitswelt, Wiesbaden 2010, pp. 53-68.

[11] Salas, Eduardo/Rico, Ramón/Passmore, Jonathan (eds.): The Wiley Blackwell Handbook of the Psychology of Team Working and Collaborative Processes, West Sussex 2017.

[12] Adler, Nancy J.: International Dimensions of Organizational Behavior, 5th ed., Mason 2008 (2002).

[13] Brenner, Doris: Onboarding. Als Führungskraft neue Mitarbeiter erfolgreich einarbeiten und integrieren, 2nd ed., Wiesbaden 2020 (2014).

[14] Galais, Nathalie/Moser, Klaus et al.: Onboarding. Neue Mitarbeiter integrieren, Göttingen 2018.

[15] Grotzfeld, Svenja/Haub, Christine/Mentzel, Wolfgang: Mitarbeitergespräche erfolgreich führen. Einzelgespräche, Teamgespräche, Zielvereinbarungen und Mitarbeiterbeurteilungen, 12th ed., Freiburg 2017.

[16] Ellis, Neil/Sampson, Helen: Seafarers' mental health and wellbeing, Leicestershire 2019, p. 9.

[17] n.a. (2020): Globaler Arbeitsmarkt für Seeleute, online: https://www.forschungs informationssystem.de/servlet/is/18458/.

[18] Marinekommando (ed.): Jahresbericht 2020. Fakten und Zahlen zur maritimen Abhängigkeit der Bundesrepublik Deutschland, Rostock 2020, p. 168.

[19] Schellbach, Annika: Die Bedeutung der Diversität von Personal an Bord von Seeschiffen, Emden/Leer 2015, p. 84.

[20] n.a. (n.d.): The IMO, online: https://www.itfglobal.org/en/sector/seafarers/ the-imo.

[21] Gerstenberger, in: Becke/Bleses/Ritter/Schmidt (2010), p. 57.

[22] n.a. (n.d.): Stiftung Schifffahrtsstandort Deutschland, online: https://www.stift ung-schifffahrtsstandort.de/.

[23] VDR (n.d.): Daten & Fakten zur Seeschifffahrt in Deutschland, online: https://www.reederverband.de/daten-und-fakten/infopool.html. The Paris MoU aims "to eliminate the operation of sub-standard ships through a harmonized system of port State control." (n.a. (n.d.): Organisation, online: https://www.parismou.org/about-us/organisation).

[24] Marinekommando (2020), p. 38.

[25] Ellis/Sampson (2019), p. 10.

[26] Marinekommando (2020), pp. 120f.

[27] Very few countries provide for interdisciplinary training. With the exception of ship mechanics, who can be employed both as motorman and A.B., there is also a strong distinction in Germany between nautical and technical careers. According to the author, this means that there is often little cooperation between the two areas and that tensions arise from ignorance of the other area.

[28] Ellis/Sampson (2019), p. 26.

[29] MacLachlan, Malcolm: Maritime Psychology. Definition, Scope and Conceptualization, in: MacLachlan (2017), p. 8.

[30] ibid., pp. 8f.

[31] ibid., p. 10.

[32] ibid., pp. 10f.

[33] ibid., p. 11.

[34] Lefkowitz/Slade (2019), p. 18.

[35] ibid., p. 5.

[36] ibid., p. 19.

[37] Jensen, Hans-Joachim/Oldenburg, Marcus: Merchant seafaring: a changing and hazardous occupation, in: Occupational and Environmental Medicine, Vol. 69, 9/2012, p. 687.

[38] In the following: Jensen/Oldenburg (2012), p. 686f.

[39] Mast, Bjorn: Depressed at Sea. A study into the mental health of seafarers, Baltic Sea 2020, p. 51.

[40] Grech/Horberry/Koester (2008), pp. 71f.

[41] ITF (2016), p. 10.

[42] ibid., p. 5.

[43] ibid., p. 5.

[44] See Qiuli, Hui: Prevention and Treatment of Occupational Diseases of Ocean Seafarers by Sports Based on Big Data, in: Journal of Coastal Research, 94/2019, p. 777.

[45] Ellis/Sampson (2019), p. 3.

[46] Jensen, Hans-Joachim/ Oldenburg, Marcus (2019): Maritime welfare facilities - utilization and relevance for the compensation of shipboard stress, in: https://occup-med.biomedcentral.com/articles/10.1186/s12995-019-0231-3, n.p.

[47] ibid., pp. 6f.

[48] ibid., p. 7.

[49] ibid., p. 5.

[50] Ellis/Sampson (2019), p. 3. In May 2022, the long-standing demand will be met and the ITF will be able to declare the right to internet for seafarers enshrined in the MLC. (See ITF (2022): Seafarers win commitment to mandatory internet access in international law, online: https://www.itfglobal.org/en/news/seafarers-win-commitment-mandatory-internet-access-in-international-law)

[51] Lefkowitz/Slade (2019), p. 19.

[52] Vaupel, Claudia: Stress, accidents and fatigue, in: Neff (2020), p. 95.

[53] The Swedish study by Bjorn Mast in the course of his bachelor's thesis is highly topical (2020) and should therefore not be completely neglected. However, only 119 (66 officers, 53 rankings) responded to his question to over 490 active seafarers. Furthermore, his question "What makes you sad when being on board?" should be considered in a differentiated way, as a feeling of sadness is not automatically attributable to depression.

[54] Grech/Horberry/Koester (2008), p. 83.

[55] ibid., p. 83.

[56] ibid., pp. 83f.

[57] ibid., pp. 84f.

[58] ibid., S. 84.

[59] ibid., S. 87.

[60] ibid., p. 11.

[61] ibid., p. 12.

[62] ITF (2016), p. 12.

[63] Fostervold/Koren/Nilsen: Defining Sustainable and "Decent" Work for Human Factors and Ergonomics, in: Thatcher, Andrew/Yeow, Paul H. P. (eds.): Ergonomics and Human Factors for a Sustainable Future. Current Research and Future Possibilities, Singapore 2018, p. 47. In this regard, Grech et al. note that the terms are to be used synonymously, but that simultaneous use has nevertheless become established. (Grech/Horberry/Koester (2008), p. 11).

[64] Becke/Bleses/Ritter/Schmidt: "Decent Work" als Leitidee im Werk von Eva Senghaas-Knobloch, in: Becke/Bleses/Ritter/Schmidt (2010), p. 10.

[65] Senghaas-Knobloch, Eva: "Decent Work" – eine weltweite Agenda für Forschung und Politik, in: Becke/Bleses/Ritter/Schmidt (2010), p. 25.

[66] ibid., p. 25. Author translation. Original: "Die gegenwärtige Situation, dass ein Teil der für die Besatzung an Bord geltenden Regeln für alle gleichermaßen gültig ist, aber ein anderer Teil, besonders der für Löhne und für Sozialschutz, je nach Nationalität der Besatzungsmitglieder von der Nationalität abhängt, macht ordnungspolitisch Schiffe zu einem besonderen Ort."

[67] Gerstenberger, in: Becke/Bleses/Ritter/Schmidt (2010), p. 67.

[68] Senghaas-Knobloch, in: Becke/Bleses/Ritter/Schmidt (2010), p. 25; Gerstenberger, in: Becke/Bleses/Ritter/ Schmidt (2010), p. 67.

[69] Schellbach (2015), p. 82.

[70] Grech/Horberry/Koester (2008), p. 18.

[71] Gerstenberger, in: Becke/Bleses/Ritter/Schmidt (2010), pp. 64f.

[72] Adler (2008), pp. 199+219.

[73] Dünnebier, Guido: Institutionen im Wandel. Ein Blick auf Diversity in der Wirtschaft, in: Fereidooni, Karim/Zeoli, Antonietta P. (eds.): Managing Diversity. Die diversitätsbewusste Ausrichtung des Bildungs- und Kulturwesens, der Wirtschaft und Verwaltung, Wiesbaden 2016, p. 342.

[74] Gutting, Doris: Diversity Management: In der Realität angekommen, in: Au, Corinna von (ed.): Führung im Zeitalter von Veränderung und Diversity. Innovationen, Change, Merger, Vielfalt und Trennung, Wiesbaden 2017, p. 155.

[75] Hanappi-Egger, Edeltraud/Hofmann, Roswitha, in: Bendl, Regine/Hanappi-Egger, Edeltraud/Hofmann, Roswitha (eds.): Diversität und Diversitätsmanagement, Vienna 2012, pp. 342f.

[76] ibid., p. 344.

[77] Hanappi-Egger, Edeltraud: Kompetenzerfordernisse im Diversity Management: zwischen Selbsterkenntnis und Fachwissen, in: Genkova, Petia/Ringeisen, Tobias (eds.): Handbuch Diversity Kompetenz. Band 1: Perspektiven und Anwendungsfelder, Wiesbaden 2016, pp. 372f.

[78] Becker, Manfred: Was ist Diversity Management?, in: Fereidooni/Zeoli (2016), p. 304.

[79] ibid, p. 300.

[80] ibid, p. 294.

[81] ibid, p. 302.

[82] Schellbach (2015), p. 22.

[83] ibid., pp. 40f.

[84] Landon, Lauren/Vessey, William: Team Performance in Extreme Environments, in: Salas/Rico/Passmore (2017), p. 532.

[85] Gutting, in: Au (2017), p. 154.

[86] Becker, in: Fereidooni/Zeoli (2016), pp. 313f.

[87] Adler (2008), p. 140.

[88] Endres, Sigrid/Weibler, Jürgen: Plural Leadership. Eine zukunftsweisende Alternative zur One-Man-Show, Wiesbaden 2019, p. 13.

[89] Adler (2008), p. 142.

[90] Hermann, Anett: Diversitätsmanagement im Team, in: Bendl/Hanappi-Egger/Hofmann (2012), p. 269. Author translation. Original: "Teams zeichnen sich [...] durch selbstbestimmte Kooperation und einen entsprechend großen Handlungsspielraum aus. [...] In Teams arbeiten Personen zusammen, die stark aufgabenbezogen aneinandergekoppelt sind, sich durch kontinuierliche Interaktion, Kooperation und bewussten Umgang mit Konflikten auszeichnen und ein gemeinsames Ziel verfolgen. Dabei sind Gleichwertigkeit und Vertrauen eine Voraussetzung."

[91] ibid., p. 265.

[92] ibid., p. 267.

[93] ibid., p. 269.

[94] ibid, p. 268.

[95] Cf. Brodbeck, Felix C./Schulz-Hardt, Stefan: Gruppenleistung und Führung, in: Hewstone, M./Jonas, K./Stroebe, W. (eds.): Sozialpsychologie, Heidelberg 2014, p. 472.

[96] Schulz-Hardt/Brodbeck (2014), pp. 473f.

[97] Landon/Vessey, in: Salas/Rico/Passmore (2017), p. 532.

[98] Hermann, in: Bendl/Hanappi-Egger/Hofmann (2012), p. 279.

[99] ibid., pp. 279-281.

[100] ibid., p. 280.

[101] ibid., p. 281.

[102] Schulz Hardt/Brodbeck (2014), p. 503

[103] Adler (2008), pp. 134f.

[104] ibid., p. 135.

[105] ibid., p. 138.

[106] ibid., p. 135.

[107] ibid., p. 136.

[108] ibid, p. 137.

[109] Adler (2008), p. 140.

[110] ibid., p. 140.

[111] Hermann, in: Bendl/Hanappi-Egger/Hofmann (2012), p. 287. Author translation. Original: "Dazu zählen Feedbackprozesse, eine klar definierte Fehlerkultur, transparente Informationsflüsse, regelmäßige Review-Prozesse und Möglichkeiten zur Mitbestimmung. Nur so können Lernprozesse und kontinuierliche Verbesserungen initiiert werden."

[112] Adler (2008), p. 47.

[113] ibid., p. 57.

[114] ibid., pp. 54ff.

[115] Landon/Vessey, in: Salas/Rico/Passmore (2017), pp. 539f.

[116] ibid., p. 540.

[117] ibid., p. 540.

[118] Werther, Simon: Shared Leadership, in: Au, Corinna von (ed.): Wirksame und nachhaltige Führungsansätze. System, Beziehung, Haltung und Individualität, Wiesbaden 2016, p. 172. Author translation. Original: "Führung als Rolle ist an eine Person gebunden, die somit die Führungsrolle ausübt. Im Gegensatz dazu ist Führung als sozialer Prozess durch mehrere Personen gekennzeichnet, so dass keine eindeutige Rollenzuordnung möglich ist."

[119] Kortmann, Olaf: 30 Minuten. Transformationales Führen, Offenbach 2016, pp. 23f.

[120] ibid., pp. 24f.

[121] ibid., p. 40.

[122] See Jeromin, Justus: Theorie und Praxis von Leadership-Konzepten mit reduzierten Hierarchien, in: Jeromin, Justus/Jourdan, Gabriel/Nell, Filippa von: Leadership in Organisationen mit reduzierten Hierarchien. Praxiswissen für die Führungsaufgabe, Wiesbaden 2018, p. 4.

[123] Kortmann (2016), p. 43.

[124] Pelz, Waldemar: Transformationale Führung – Forschungsstand und Umsetzung in der Praxis, in: Au (2016), p. 94.

[125] Pelz, in: Au (2016), p. 109. Author Translation. Original: "Er (oder sie) meint, was er sagt" – "Steht für klare Wertvorstellungen" – "Setzt klare Ziele und Erwartungen" – "Verfügt über profunde Fachkenntnisse ("Breite" vs. "Tiefe")" - "Ist offen für Kritik und neue Ideen" – "Man kann sich auf ihn/sie verlassen" - "Verhält sich in einer Weise, die Respekt verdient"

[126] ibid., p. 110.

[127] Kortmann (2016), pp. 52f.

[128] ibid., pp. 59f.

[129] ibid., p. 67.

[130] ibid., pp. 78f.

[131] ibid., p. 86.

[132] Mödler, Beate: Arbeitsbeziehungs- und Organisationsaufstellungen zur Visualisierung und Reflexion komplexe Führungssituationen, in: Mödler, Beate/Schürkamp, Michael/ Siebenbrock, Heinz u.a.: Führen Sie schon oder herrschen Sie noch? Faires Management - der Methodenband, Marburg 2016, p. 128. Author translation. Original: "Arbeitsbeziehungen erscheinen so selbstverständlich, dass sie meist erst dann wahrgenommen werden, wenn es zu Konflikten kommt."

[133] Mödler, in: Siebenbrock (2016), p. 156.

[134] ibid., p. 158.

[135] ibid., p. 188.

[136] Kortmann (2016), p. 71.

[137] Happel, Herbert: Hierarchie als Chance. Für erfolgreiche Kommunikation und Kooperation in Team und Organisation, Wiesbaden 2017, p. 5.

[138] ibid., p. 6.

[139] Endres/Weibler (2019), p. 13.

[140] Happel (2017), pp. 210ff.

[141] ibid., p. 210.

[142] ibid., p. 211. Author translation. Original: "'Organisationsbewusstsein' über den eigenen Platz in der Hierarchie hilft, zu unterscheiden zwischen gleichberechtigtem Diskutieren, Verhandeln, Beraten auf der einen Seite und dem Anweisen, Delegieren, Sich-Beraten-Lassen in komplementären Rollen auf der anderen Seite."

[143] ibid., p. 211.

[144] Happel (2017), p. 211.

[145] ibid., p. 215. Author translation. Original: "Ein fortdauernder grenzenloser Missbrauch von Hierarchie und Struktur zum Schaden des Einzelnen aber – so meine positive Sicht und Zuversicht – wird aus dem Selbstverständnis, der Sachdienlichkeit und der Überlebensstrategie der Organisation heraus auf Dauer keinen Bestand haben. Denn dann kommt es zu Störungen in der Aufgabenerfüllung und, über Rückmeldeschleifen, zu Veränderungen in Richtung des Überlebens der Einrichtung, der Weiterentwicklung und einer positiven Nutzung der Hierarchie."

[146] Maritime Labour Organization (MLC) provides for a protected "on-board complaints procedure" (see MLC 5.1.5). However, these regulations are almost undermined by the fact that the captain is designated as the address for complaints

by the crew, who can be biased on several levels. (n.a. (2014): Right to complain on board, online: https://seafarersrights.org/right-to-complain-on-board/.)

[147] Landon/Vessey, in: Salas/Rico/Passmore (2017), p. 541.

[148] Endres/Weibler (2019), p. 14.

[149] ibid., p. 15.

[150] Endres/Weibler (2019), p. 10.

[151] ibid., p. 11.

[152] ibid., p. 30.

[153] ibid., p. 42.

[154] ibid., p. 26.

[155] Jung, Thomas: Aspects of Leadership and Teamwork, in: Neff (2020), p. 212.

[156] ibid., S. 212.

[157] ibid., p. 212.

[158] ibid., p. 221.

[159] ibid., p. 233.

[160] Neff, Jürgen: Team spirit and group dynamics, in: Neff (2020), p. 207.

[161] ibid., p. 208.

[162] ibid., pp. 208f.

[163] Gesing, Sophia/Weber, Ulrike: Feelgood Management. Chancen für etablierte Unternehmen, Wiesbaden 2019, p. 9.

[164] Siebenbrock, Heinz: Faires Management in der Praxis, in: Mödler/Schürkamp/Siebenbrock et al. (2016), p. 216.

[165] Gesing/Weber (2019), p. 14.

[166] In such watch systems, the 24 hours of a day are divided into six or four shifts, which are performed by three or two people respectively. During port lay times or manoeuvres (river cruises, port entrances), this rhythm often becomes obsolete again.

[167] Gesing, Sophia/Weber, Ulrike: Konzept und Berufsbild des Feelgood-Managements, Wiesbaden 2017, p. 24.

[168] ibid., p. 37.

[169] ibid., p. 33.

[170] Gesing/Weber (2019), p. 16.

[171] ibid., p. 16.

[172] Gesing/Weber (2019)., p. 31. Author translation. Original: "Anstelle von hierarchischer Macht tritt die Notwendigkeit von lateraler und partizipativer Führung, die Kooperation und Vertrauen stärkt."

[173] Siebenbrock, in: Siebenbrock (2016), p. 26.

[174] Galais/Moser et al. (2018), p. 1.

[175] ibid., p. 2.

[176] Brenner, p. 12.

[177] Galais/Moser et al. (2018), p. 48.

[178] ibid., p. 55.

[179] ibid., pp. 56ff.

[180] Brenner (2020), pp. 9f.

[181] ibid., p. 23.

[182] ibid., p. 35.

[183] ibid., p. 16.

[184] ibid., pp. 20f.

[185] Galais/Moser et al. (2018), p. 1.

[186] Neuberger, Oswald: Das Mitarbeitergespräch. Praktische Grundlagen für erfolgreiche Führungsarbeit, 6th ed., Wiesbaden 2015 (Leonberg, 2004), p. 8.

[187] Grotzfeld/Haub/Mentzel (2017), p. 17. Author translation. Original: "Zum Mitarbeitergespräch zählen alle Gespräche zwischen Vorgesetzten und ihren Mitarbeitern, die über die routinemäßige Alltagskommunikation hinausgehen. [...] Mitarbeitergespräche sind Führungsaufgaben und daher nicht delegierbar."

[188] Alter, Urs: Grundlagen der Kommunikation für Führungskräfte. Mitarbeitende informieren und Führungsgespräche erfolgreich durchführen, 2nd ed., Wiesbaden 2018 (2015), p. 14.

[189] Grotzfeld/Haub/Mentzel (2017), p. 13.

[190] ibid., p. 27. Author translation. Original: "Das Mitarbeitergespräch ist ein Zweckgespräch, das mit einer ganz bestimmten Absicht geführt wird."

[191] ibid., p. 51.

[192] ibid., p. 52.

[193] ibid., pp. 109ff.

[194] ibid., p. 65.

[195] ibid., p. 82.

[196] ibid., p. 83.

[197] Grotzfeld/Haub/Mentzel (2017)., p. 57. Author translation. Original: "Inhaltlich hat das Beurteilungsgespräch viel mit dem Feedbackgespräch gemeinsam. In beiden Fällen geht es darum, gute Leistungen anzuerkennen und schlechte Leistungen zu verbessern. […] Während es sich beim Feedbackgespräch um eine Momentaufnahme handelt, entfaltet das Beurteilungsgespräch weitreichende Konsequenzen."

[198] ibid., p. 56.

[199] Neuberger (2015), pp. 190f.

[200] ibid., p. 191.

[201] ibid., p. 194.

[202] ibid., pp. 194ff.

[203] ibid., pp. 195f.

[204] ibid., p. 197. Author translation. Original: "Die Kritik entwickelt sich dann zum routinemäßigen Ritual, bei dem der Mitarbeiter seine Unterwerfung demonstriert und noch einmal davonkommt, ohne dass sich langfristig etwas ändert. Anerkennung und Kritik werden dann als Mittel gesehen, die bestehenden hierarchischen Distanzen zu markieren und zu konservieren."

[205] ibid., pp. 203+208.

[206] Neuberger (2015), p. 209.

[207] ibid., pp. 212+220.

[208] ibid., pp. 214+219.

[209] ibid., p. 224.

[210] Grotzfeld/Haub/Mentzel (2017), p. 159.

[211] Achouri, Cyrus: Human Resources Management. Eine praxisbasierte Einführung, Wiesbaden 2011, p. 157.

[212] ibid., p. 158.

[213] Nerdinger, Friedemann W.: Vorgesetztenbeurteilung, in: Bungard, Walter/Jöns, Ingela (eds.): Feedbackinstrumente im Unternehmen. Grundlagen, Gestaltungshinweise, Erfahrungsberichte, 2nd ed., Wiesbaden 2018 (2005), pp. 109f.

[214] ibid., pp. 113+116f.

[215] ibid., p. 117.

[216] Cox/Doyle/Dyer et al.: Positive Psychology and Well-Being at Sea, in: MacLachlan (2017), p. 21.

[217] Chialing, Yao/Paichin, Huang: Effects of Leadership Style on Job Satisfaction and Intention to Stay in Shipping Industry, in: Journal of Coastal Research, 83/2018, p. 796.

REFERENCES

ACHOURI, CYRUS: Human Resources Management. Eine praxisbasierte Einführung, Wiesbaden 2011.

ADLER, NANCY J.: International Dimensions of Organizational Behavior, 5th ed., Mason 2008 (2002).

ALTER, URS: Grundlagen der Kommunikation für Führungskräfte. Mitarbeitende informieren und Führungsgespräche erfolgreich durchführen, 2nd ed., Wiesbaden 2018 (2015).

AU, CORINNA VON (ed.): Führung im Zeitalter von Veränderung und Diversity. Innovationen, Change, Merger, Vielfalt und Trennung, Wiesbaden 2017.

AU, CORINNA VON (ed.): Wirksame und nachhaltige Führungsansätze. System, Beziehung, Haltung und Individualität, Wiesbaden 2016.

BECKE, GUIDO/BLESES, PETER/RITTER, WOLFGANG/SCHMIDT, SANDRA (eds.): "Decent Work". Arbeitspolitische Gestaltungsperspektive für eine globalisierte und flexibilisierte Arbeitswelt, Wiesbaden 2010.

BENDL, REGINE/HANAPPI-EGGER, EDELTRAUD/HOFMANN, ROSWITHA (eds.): Diversität und Diversitätsmanagement, Wien 2012.

BORCH, DANIEL/BURR, HERMANN/HANSEN, HENRIK/JEPSEN, JOERGEN: Surveillance of maritime deaths on board Danish merchant ships, 1986–2009, in: International Maritime Health, 1/2012, pp. 7-16.

BRENNER, DORIS: Onboarding. Als Führungskraft neue Mitarbeiter erfolgreich einarbeiten und integrieren, 2nd ed., Wiesbaden 2020 (2014).

BRODBECK, FELIX C./SCHULZ-HARDT, STEFAN: Gruppenleistung und Führung, in: Hewstone, M./Jonas, K./Stroebe, W. (eds.): Sozialpsychologie, Heidelberg 2014, pp. 469-505.

BUNGARD, WALTER/JÖNS, INGELA (eds.): Feedbackinstrumente im Unternehmen. Grundlagen, Gestaltungshinweise, Erfahrungsberichte, 2nd ed., Wiesbaden 2018 (2005).

CHIALING, YAO/PAICHIN, HUANG: Effects of Leadership Style on Job Satisfaction and Intention to Stay in Shipping Industry, in: Journal of Coastal Research, 83/2018, pp. 796-801.

ELLIS, NEIL/SAMPSON, HELEN: Seafarers' mental health and wellbeing, Leicestershire 2019.

ENDRES, SIGRID/WEIBLER, JÜRGEN: Plural Leadership. Eine zukunftsweisende Alternative zur One-Man-Show, Wiesbaden 2019.

FEREIDOONI, KARIM/ZEOLI, ANTONIETTA P. (eds.): Managing Diversity. Die diversitätsbewusste Ausrichtung des Bildungs- und Kulturwesens, der Wirtschaft und Verwaltung, Wiesbaden 2016.

GALAIS, NATHALIE/MOSER, KLAUS et al: Onboarding. Neue Mitarbeiter integrieren, Göttingen 2018.

GENKOVA, PETIA/RINGEISEN, TOBIAS (eds.): Handbuch Diversity Kompetenz. Band 1: Perspektiven und Anwendungsfelder, Wiesbaden 2016.

GESING, SOPHIA/WEBER, ULRIKE: Feelgood-Management. Chancen für etablierte Unternehmen, Wiesbaden 2019.

GESING, SOPHIA/WEBER, ULRIKE: Konzept und Berufsbild des Feelgood-Managements, Wiesbaden 2017.

GRECH, MICHELLE R./HORBERRY, TIM J./KOESTER, THOMAS: Human factors in the maritime domain, Boca Raton 2008.

GROTZFELD, SVENJA/HAUB, CHRISTINE/ MENTZEL, WOLFGANG: Mitarbeitergespräche erfolgreich führen. Einzelgespräche, Teamgespräche, Zielvereinbarungen und Mitarbeiterbeurteilungen, 12th ed., Freiburg 2017.

HAPPEL, HERBERT: Hierarchie als Chance. Für erfolgreiche Kommunikation und Kooperation in Team und Organisation, Wiesbaden 2017.

HARTH, V./HERZOG, J./OLDENBURG, M.: Seafarer deaths at sea: a German mortality study, in: Occupational Medicine, 66/2016, pp. 135-137.

ITF (2022): Seafarers win commitment to mandatory internet access in international law, online: https://www.itfglobal.org/en/news/seafarers-win-commitment-mandatory-internet-access-in-international-law.

ITF: Summary report from the ITF Seafarers' Trust Autumn 2016 workshop on Social Isolation Depression and Suicide (SIDS), n.a. 2016.

JENSEN, HANS-JOACHIM/ OLDENBURG, MARCUS (2019): Maritime welfare facilities – utilization and relevance for the compensation of shipboard stress, online: https://occup-med.biomedcentral.com/articles/10.1186/s12995-019-0231-3.

JENSEN, HANS-JOACHIM/OLDENBURG, MARCUS: Merchant seafaring: a changing and hazardous occupation, in: Occupational and Environmental Medicine, Vol. 69, 9/2012, pp. 685-688.

JEROMIN, JUSTUS/JOURDAN, GABRIEL/NELL, FILIPPA VON: Leadership in Organisationen mit reduzierten Hierarchien. Praxiswissen für die Führungsaufgabe, Wiesbaden 2018.

KORTMANN, OLAF: 30 Minuten. Transformationales Führen, Offenbach 2016.

KRUECKEN, STEFAN (2020): SOS an Heiligabend, online: https://www.spiegel.de/karriere/seeleute-in-der-corona-krise-s-o-s-an-heiligabend-a-195be52b-0634-460b-aa7f-46231a6353a7.

LEFKOWITZ, RAFAEL Y./SLADE, MARTIN D.: Seafarer Mental Health Study, London 2019.

MACLACHLAN, MALCOLM (ed.): Maritime Psychology. Research in Organizational & Health Behavior at Sea, Cham 2017.

MARINEKOMMANDO (ed.): Jahresbericht 2020. Fakten und Zahlen zur maritimen Abhängigkeit der Bundesrepublik Deutschland, Rostock 2020.

MAST, BJORN: Depressed at Sea. A study into the mental health of seafarers, Baltic Sea 2020.

MÖDLER, BEATE/SCHÜRKAMP, MICHAEL/SIEBENBROCK, HEINZ u.a.: Führen Sie schon oder herrschen Sie noch? Faires Management - der Methodenband, Marburg 2016.

n.a. (2014): Right to complain on board, online: https://seafarersrig hts.org/right-to-complain-on-board/.

n.a. (2020): Globaler Arbeitsmarkt für Seeleute, online: https://www.forschungsinformationssystem.de/servlet/is/18458/.

n.a. (n.a.): Organisation, online: https://www.parismou.org/about-us/organisation.

n.a. (n.a.): Stiftung Schifffahrtsstandort Deutschland, online: https://www.stiftung-schifffahrtsstandort.de/.

n.a. (n.a.): The IMO, online: https://www.itfglobal.org/ en/sector/seafarers/the-imo.

NEFF, JÜRGEN (Hrsg.): Improving Bridge Resource Management. Human Factors in Maritime Safety, Leverkusen 2020.

NEUBERGER, OSWALD: Das Mitarbeitergespräch. Praktische Grundlagen für erfolgreiche Führungsarbeit, 6. ed., Wiesbaden 2015 (Leonberg, 2004).

QIULI, HUI: Prevention and Treatment of Occupational Diseases of Ocean Seafarers by Sports Based on Big Data, in: Journal of Coastal Research, 94/2019, pp. 773-777.

SALAS, EDUARDO/RICO, RAMÓN/PASSMORE, JONATHAN (eds.): The Wiley Blackwell Handbook of the Psychology of Team Working and Collaborative Processes, West Sussex 2017.

SCHELLBACH, ANNIKA: Die Bedeutung der Diversität von Personal an Bord von Seeschiffen, Emden/Leer 2015.

THATCHER, ANDREW/YEOW, PAUL H. P. (eds.): Ergonomics and Human Factors for a Sustainable Future. Current Research and Future Possibilities, Singapore 2018.

VDR (n.a.): Daten & Fakten zur Seeschifffahrt in Deutschland, online: https://www.reederverband.de/daten-und-fakten/infopool.html.

WADEL, CARL C.: Interaction and Risk Management in Shared Leadership, in: Torgersen, G.-E, (ed.): Interaction: 'Samhandling' Under Risk. A Step Ahead of the Unforeseen, Oslo 2018, pp. 233-250.